Conquer Grammar

Table of Contents

Introduction 5

Nouns
Singular and Plural Nouns 8
Irregular Plural Nouns 9
Abstract Nouns 10
Concrete and Abstract Nouns 11
Possessive Nouns 14

Verbs
Past Tense Verbs 20
Verb Tenses 22
Irregular Past Tense Verbs 24
Irregular and Regular Past Tense Verbs 30
Irregular Verbs: **to be** and **have** 31

Subject-Verb Agreement
Subject-Verb Agreement 32

Pronouns
Subject and Object Pronouns 36
Pronoun-Antecedent Agreement 37
Possessive Pronouns 39
Indefinite Pronouns 40
Reflexive Pronouns 41
Reciprocal Pronouns 42

Adjectives and Adverbs
Adjectives 45
Adverbs 47
Adjectives and Adverbs 49
Comparatives 52
Superlatives 53
Comparatives and Superlatives 54

Prepositions and Conjunctions
Prepositions 59
Conjunctions 62

Punctuation
Commas for Greetings and Closings 63
End Marks 64
Contractions 66
Punctuate Dialogue 68

Capitalization
Capitalize Proper Nouns 73
Capitalize Book Titles 75

Sentences
Sentence Types 76
Fragments and Complete Sentences 77
Use Coordinating Conjunctions to Form
Compound Sentences 79
Use Subordinating Conjunctions to Form
Complex Sentences 82
Compound and Complex Sentences 85

Language
Standard English 90

Answer Key 92

Introduction

This book is designed to help students have a better understanding of grammar, the fundamental organizing principle of language. The standards for most states as well as the Common Core State Standards require that students "Demonstrate command of the conventions of standard English grammar usage when writing and speaking." Students who understand how to use proper grammar are better able to say what they mean when writing and speaking.

Each of the 84 worksheets in this book reinforces a grade-appropriate grammar topic. The book is organized by parts of speech and other key topics. The goal is to equip students with an understanding of grammar so they can communicate more effectively.

How to Use This Book

Here are just a few of the many ways you can use this resource.

Grammar Mini-Lessons: The most basic way to use this book is as a source of grammar mini-lessons. Write the grammar rule on the board. You can copy this straight from the gray box found on each worksheet. Introduce the rule, explain it, and then give examples. See if students can come up with their own examples. Then have students complete the worksheet. You can ask students to complete the worksheets individually or with partners, depending on ability levels. Check for understanding.

Grammar Reinforcement: After you have taught students a particular grammar rule, you can use these pages to give students the practice they need to reinforce their knowledge of the skill.

Grammar Assessment: The worksheets can serve as a formative assessment tool to show you where students might need additional teaching. Worksheets can also serve as a final assessment to confirm that students have mastered a particular rule.

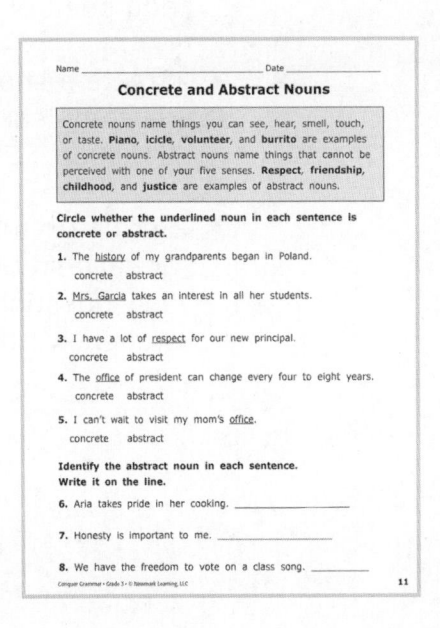

Beyond the Book

There are myriad ways in which you can extend the lessons in this book. The goal is to keep the learning fun and interactive. Here are several ideas to get you started.

- Find examples of grammar rules you are studying in books you are reading in class. Point out these examples to students. Then send students on a scavenger hunt to find examples themselves. You can expand the search area to books students read at home and in magazines, newspapers, notices around school, advertisements—anywhere there is a written word. The more places students see the rule being used, the better.

- Ask students to practice using specific grammar rules in their own writing. For example, if you are studying a particular type of punctuation, have students use that punctuation in their writing. They can even go back and revise old work using, knowledge gained from new grammar rules.

- Build a grammar "Wall of Shame" where you post examples of writing—usually from advertisements—where grammar rules were ignored, often to humorous effect. Encourage students to look for examples to add to the Wall of Shame. You might want to post an example you can easily find on the Internet, "Let's eat Grandpa" versus "Let's eat, Grandpa," and point out that grammar can save lives.

- Create a short daily exercise in which students are asked to use a recently learned grammar rule to correct a sentence that is written on the board. Students love correcting others' mistakes!

- Set up grammar stations with worksheets that cover a different rule at each station. Have students work in small groups to add one or two new questions to the worksheet at each station. Make a quiz out of the student-written questions.

Key Tips for Teaching English Learners

The rules of grammar vary between different languages. This can make learning English grammar particularly difficult for English Learners. It is helpful to know where the grammar rules between languages differ so much as to cause a fair amount of confusion. Here are some of those areas.

Word Order	In languages such as Spanish, Farsi, Arabic, and Korean, word order in sentences may vary from that of English.
Verbs	In English, verbs are inflected for person and number. (*Everyone cooks food. She has a large cat.*) In Vietnamese, Hmong, Korean, Cantonese, and Mandarin, verbs are not inflected for person and number. (*Everyone cook food. She have large cat.*)
Nouns	Nouns and adjectives use different forms in English. (*They felt safe in their home. They were concerned about safety.*) In Spanish, Hmong, Cantonese, and Mandarin, speakers use the same form for nouns and adjectives. (*They felt safety in their home.*)
Possessive Nouns	In English, we add an apostrophe and *s* to most singular nouns, or an apostrophe only to proper, plural names that end in *s*, to show possession. In Spanish, Vietnamese, Hmong, and Tagalog, possession is shown using *of*. It is always *of Holly*, not *Holly's*.
Plural Nouns	Nouns become plural after a number greater than one in English. (*We go home in two weeks. They are bringing five shirts.*) In Vietnamese, Hmong, Tagalog, Korean, Cantonese, Mandarin, and Farsi, there is no change in the noun following a number. (*We go home in two week. They are bringing five shirt.*)
Adjectives	Adjectives precede the nouns they modify in English (*the blue flower*). In Spanish, Vietnamese, Hmong, Farsi, and Arabic, adjectives follow the nouns they modify (*the flower blue*).
Pronouns	In English, there is a distinction between subject and object pronouns. (*He gave it to me. We spent time with her.*) In Spanish, Vietnamese, Hmong, Cantonese, Mandarin, and Farsi, there is no distinction. (*He gave it to I. We spent time with she.*)
Prepositions	The use of prepositions in other languages differs from the use of prepositions in English. (English: *The movie is on the DVD.* Spanish: *The movie is in the DVD.*)
Articles	Indefinite articles are used consistently in English. (*She is a brilliant scientist. He is an electrician.*) In Spanish, Hmong, Tagalog, Cantonese, and Mandarin, indefinite articles can be omitted. (*She is brilliant scientist. He is electrician.*)

Name _____ Date _____

Singular and Plural Nouns

A singular noun names a person, place, or thing. A plural noun names more than one person, place, or thing. Add **s** to the end of most nouns to make them plural.

Singular Noun	**Plural Noun**
student	students
lesson	lessons
notebook	notebooks

Circle the noun that correctly completes each sentence. Write it on the line.

1. Our teacher asked us to take out a sheet of _____.

   (paper, papers)

2. There are two _____ in this school who are named Mr. Smith!

   (teacher, teachers)

3. She used brown and green _____ to add trees to her picture.

   (marker, markers)

4. My favorite _____ is written by Beverly Cleary.

   (book, books)

5. Mrs. Taylor has extra _____ in a basket if we need to borrow one of them.

   (pencil, pencils)

Name _____   Date _____

Irregular Plural Nouns

A plural noun names more than one person, place, or thing. Regular plural nouns end in **s**. Irregular plural nouns do not have any spelling rules or patterns. Some examples of nouns and their irregular plural forms include **goose/geese, foot/feet,** and **ox/oxen**.

Complete each sentence with the plural form of the noun in the parentheses ( ).

1. How many _____ are going to the party? (person)

2. Annie has two pet _____ named Lola and Daisy. (mouse)

3. The _____ were splashing in the swimming pool. (woman)

4. Those _____ are talking about the same book. (child)

5. Are you waiting for any baby _____ to fall out? (tooth)

6. My dad and the other _____ cheered the loudest. (man)

7. The flock of _____ flew over the park. (geese)

8. We saw _____ at the animal sanctuary. (wolf)

Conquer Grammar • Grade 3 • © Newmark Learning, LLC

Name _____ Date _____

Abstract Nouns

> Concrete nouns name things that you can see, hear, smell, taste, or touch. **Pizza**, **cloud**, and **friend** are examples of concrete nouns. Abstract nouns name things that cannot be perceived with one of your five senses. **Hunger**, **loyalty**, and **democracy** are examples of abstract nouns.

Choose the correct abstract noun from the box to complete each sentence. Write it on the line.

| patriotism | weather | wisdom | generosity |
| independence | vacation | pleasure | disagreements |

1. Mr. Han paid me more than he needed to. His _____ is overwhelming!

2. My family is going to the lake for _____.

3. I hope that the _____ on Tuesday will be cool and dry.

4. We march in a parade to show our _____.

5. On the Fourth of July Americans celebrate the country's _____.

6. My little sister and I have our _____ but we still love each other.

7. I like helping others and get _____ from doing it.

8. My aunt often gives me advice, she has a deep _____ about things.

Name _____   Date _____

Concrete and Abstract Nouns

> Concrete nouns name things you can see, hear, smell, touch, or taste. **Piano**, **icicle**, **volunteer**, and **burrito** are examples of concrete nouns. Abstract nouns name things that cannot be perceived with one of your five senses. **Respect**, **friendship**, **childhood**, and **justice** are examples of abstract nouns.

Circle whether the underlined noun in each sentence is concrete or abstract.

1. The <u>history</u> of my grandparents began in Poland.
    concrete   abstract

2. <u>Mrs. Garcia</u> takes an interest in all her students.
    concrete   abstract

3. I have a lot of <u>respect</u> for our new principal.
    concrete   abstract

4. The <u>office</u> of president can change every four to eight years.
    concrete   abstract

5. I can't wait to visit my mom's <u>office</u>.
    concrete   abstract

Identify the abstract noun in each sentence. Write it on the line.

6. Aria takes pride in her cooking. _____

7. Honesty is important to me. _____

8. We have the freedom to vote on a class song. _____

Conquer Grammar • Grade 3 • © Newmark Learning, LLC   11

Name _____ Date _____

Concrete and Abstract Nouns

Concrete nouns are things you can see, hear, smell, touch, or taste. **Classroom**, **teacher**, **pizza**, **music**, and **sidewalk** are examples of concrete nouns. Abstract nouns are things that cannot be perceived with one of your five senses. **Courage**, **fear**, **curiosity**, **hope**, and **kindness** are examples of abstract nouns.

Determine whether each noun in the box is concrete or abstract. Then write the noun in the correct column of the chart.

| kindness | music | rhythm | scent | shade |
| bravery | happiness | backache | writer | peace |

Concrete Nouns	Abstract Nouns

Name _____ Date _____

Concrete and Abstract Nouns

Concrete nouns name things you can see, hear, smell, touch, or taste. **Auditorium**, **sunset**, **cupcake**, and **music** are examples of concrete nouns. Abstract nouns name things that cannot be perceived with one of your five senses. **Truth**, **honesty**, **luck**, **brilliance**, and **delight** are examples of abstract nouns.

Determine whether each noun in the box is concrete or abstract. Then write the noun in the correct column of the chart.

| faith | mountains | disappointment | candidates |
| confidence | kindness | sunlight | sister |

Concrete Nouns	Abstract Nouns

Choose the correct noun from the chart above to complete each sentence. Write it on the line.

1. It was a _____ for Juan to miss the game.

2. Thank you for your _____ toward our new teammates.

3. My _____ is five years older than I am.

Name _____ Date _____

Possessive Nouns

A possessive noun tells who or what owns something.
Use **'s** to show possession for one person, place, or thing.
    Ollie's bike
Use **s'** to show possession for more than one person, place, or thing.
    our **cousins'** house
Use **'s** to show possession for nouns with irregular plural forms.
    the **women's** basketball team

Write the possessive form of each underlined noun.

1. The question of the student   the _____ question

2. the job of Mr. Wright   _____ job

3. the barking of their dogs   their _____ barking

4. the dog of your friend   Your _____ dog

5. the garden of our neighbors   our _____ garden

6. the games of the children   the _____ games

7. the cameras of those tourists   those _____ cameras

8. the meeting of the teachers   the _____ meeting

Name _____   Date _____

Possessive Nouns

> A possessive noun tells who or what owns something.
>
> Use **'s** to show possession for one person, place, or thing.
>   **Prince's** castle
>
> Use **s'** to show possession for more than one person, place, or thing.
>   **Princes'** castles
>
> Use **'s** to show possession for nouns with irregular plural forms.
>   **Women's** locker room

Write the possessive of each underlined noun.

1. the courage of the child   the _____ courage

2. the math class of Ms. Manel   _____ math class

3. the cars of your uncle   your _____ cars

4. the brother of my mother   my _____ brother

Rewrite each sentence. Replace the underlined words with a possessive.

5. The three kittens of my cat are playful.

_____

6. We replaced the batteries of our car.

_____

Name _____ Date _____

Possessive Nouns

> A possessive noun tells who or what owns something.
>
> Use **'s** to show possession for one person, place, or thing.
>   **Max's** shoes
>
> Use **s'** to show possession for more than one person, place, or thing.
>   **Flowers'** petals
>
> Use **'s** to show possession for nouns with irregular plural forms.
>   **Men's** team

Write the possessive of each underlined noun.

1. the instruments of the <u>band</u>   the _____ instruments

2. the toys of our <u>neighbors</u>   our _____ toys

3. the hobbies of some <u>people</u>   some _____ hobbies

4. the cousin of my <u>father</u>   my _____ cousin

Rewrite each sentence. Replace the underlined words with a possessive.

4. The <u>hockey team of the men</u> plays on Monday.

   _____

5. I wash the <u>manes of the horses.</u>

   _____

Name _____ Date _____

Possessive Nouns

> A possessive noun tells who or what owns something.
> Use **'s** to show possession for one person, place, or thing
>   **Billy's** shoes
>   **class's** teacher
> Use **s'** to show possession for more than one person, place, or thing.
>   **cars'** lights
> Use **'s** to show possession for nouns with irregular plural forms.
>   **Children's** home

Rewrite each sentence. Replace the underlined words with a possessive.

1. The <u>seats on the train</u> are really comfortable.

   _____

2. You can borrow <u>the skateboard that belongs to my brother</u>.

   _____

3. I walk <u>the dogs of my neighbors</u>.

   _____

4. This is the <u>table for the children</u>.

   _____

5. <u>The rules of the teachers</u> are tough but fair.

Possessive Nouns

> A possessive noun tells who or what owns something.
> Use **'s** to show possession for one person, place, or thing
>   **Ted's** coat
> Use **s'** to show possession for more than one person, place, or thing.
>   **Dancers'** shoes
> Use **'s** to show possession for nouns with irregular plural forms.
>   **Women's** team

Rewrite each sentence. Replace the underlined words with a possessive.

1. The seats in the stadium are blue and red.

   _____

2. Long ago, coats that belonged to men were fancy.

   _____

3. The mascots of the teams are different.

   _____

4. The arms of the chair are torn.

   _____

5. I found a hat belonging to Sid!

   _____

6. This is the car belonging to my cousins.

   _____

Name _____ Date _____

Possessive Nouns

> A possessive noun tells who or what owns something.
> Use **'s** to show possession for one person, place, or thing.
>   **Ginny's** sunflowers
> Use **s'** to show possession for more than one person, place, or thing.
>   our **friends'** parents
> Use **'s** to show possession for nouns with irregular plural forms.
>   the **children's** playground

Rewrite each sentence. Replace the underlined words with a possessive.

1. A father picks up <u>the toys of his toddler</u>.

   _____

2. <u>The softball team of the girls</u> practices after school.

   _____

3. <u>Clothes for men</u> are on sale in that store.

   _____

4. The kittens hid under the bed in <u>the room of Kaylee</u>.

   _____

5. <u>The kitchen of my grandmother</u> smelled of freshly baked cookies.

   _____

Name _____ Date _____

Past Tense Verbs

Past tense verbs tell about actions that already happened. Most past tense verbs end in **ed**.		
For most regular verbs, add **-ed**	spill + **ed**	spilled
If a verb ends in **e**, add **-d**	advanc**e** + **d**	advanced
If a verb ends in a vowel and a single consonant, double the consonant and add **-ed**	st**op** + **p** + **ed**	stopped
If a verb ends in a consonant and **y**, change the **y** to **i** and add **-ed**	mar**ry** mar**ri** + **ed**	married

Write the past tense form of the verb in the parentheses ( ).

1. Yesterday, Renee and I (watch) _____ the new show.

2. The baby (cry) _____ because he was hungry.

3. Were you (invite) _____ to the party?

4. I (spot) _____ my cousins in the crowd.

5. Benjamin Franklin (invent) _____ many useful things.

6. It was such a warm day that we (decide) _____ to go for a walk.

7. I am not (allow) _____ to go to the store alone.

Name _____ Date _____

Past Tense Verbs

Past tense verbs tell about actions that already happened. Most past tense verbs end in **ed**.		
For most regular verbs, add **-ed**	spill + **ed**	spilled
If a verb ends in **e**, add **-d**	advanc**e** + **d**	advanced
If a verb ends in a vowel and a single consonant, double the consonant and add **-ed**	st**op** + **p** + **ed**	stopped
If a verb ends in a consonant and **y**, change the **y** to **i** and add **-ed**	mar**ry** mar**ri** + **ed**	married

Rewrite each sentence with the past tense form of the verb in the parentheses ( ).

1. My brother (apply) to five colleges.

   _____

2. Our dad (help) him with his applications.

   _____

3. He (shout) with joy when he was accepted!

   _____

4. He (worry) that he wouldn't get in.

   _____

5. I (hug) him because I was so happy!

   _____

Name _____ Date _____

Verb Tenses

A verb is a word that shows action. Present tense verbs tell about something that is happening right now. Past tense verbs tell about something that has already happened. Future tense verbs tell about something that will happen at a later time.
Present: I **help** my family with household chores.
Past: Yesterday, I **helped** my sister sweep the garage.
Future: I **will help** my brother wash dishes.

Choose the correct verb from the box to complete each sentence. Write it on the line.

board	boarded	will board
release	released	will release
welcome	welcomed	will welcome

1. We _____ the ship over an hour ago.

2. The band _____ a new album next year.

3. Please _____ Jorge to our book club.

4. My cousins _____ a new baby in a few months.

5. I _____ the balloons into the air at the end of my birthday.

6. The passengers _____ the plane at 8:00 p.m.

Name _____ Date _____

Verb Tenses

A verb is a word that shows action. Present tense verbs tell about something that is happening right now. Past tense verbs tell about something that has already happened. Future tense verbs tell about something that will happen at a later time.

Circle the form of the verb that correctly completes each sentence. Write it on the line.

1. The baby _____ around the house.

    crawl   crawled   will crawl

2. Unless it rains, we _____ tennis later.

    play   played   will play

3. The audience must _____ at the concert hall on time.

    arrive   arrived   will arrive

Rewrite each sentence with the past tense form of the verb in the parentheses ( ).

4. I (stop) at my friend's house after school.

   _____

5. I (try) to make the cake, but it did not taste as good.

   _____

6. I (fix) the vase by gluing it together.

   _____

Conquer Grammar • Grade 3 • © Newmark Learning, LLC   23

Name _____ Date _____

Irregular Past Tense Verbs

Past tense verbs tell about actions that already happened. Past tense verbs that do not end in -**ed** are irregular.

Circle the verb in the parentheses ( ) that correctly completes each sentence.

1. My parents (buyed   bought) me a scooter for my birthday.

2. They (found   finded) the exact kind that I wanted.

3. The scooter (is   are) not new, but I love it.

4. I (growed   grew) out of my old scooter last summer.

5. Who (got   getted) your scooter for you?

6. We (is   are) both so lucky to have scooters!

7. Our friends (made   maked) us cases for our scooters.

8. I (have   had) fun riding my scooter yesterday.

9. Jenna (rided   rode) her scooter, too.

10. We (went   go) to the park for lunch.

11. We (sit   sat) on a bench and (drink   drank) water.

12. Elizabeth decided to (leave   left) early.

Name _____ Date _____

Irregular Past Tense Verbs

> Past tense verbs tell about actions that already happened. Past tense verbs that do not end in **-ed** are irregular. Some examples of verbs and their irregular past tense forms include **to be/was**, **have/had**, **find/found**, **grow/grew**, **buy/bought**, **get/got**, and **make/made**.

Circle the verb in the parentheses ( ) that correctly completes each sentence. Write it on the line.

1. My friends and I _____ banana bread yesterday. (maked, made)

2. It _____ really tasty. (was, be)

3. Kira's mom _____ the ingredients for us. (get, got)

4. She _____ almost everything at the grocery store near the mall. (bought, buyed)

5. She _____ to go to another store for the spices. (had, haved)

6. Luckily, she _____ them! (finded, found)

7. My brothers _____ happy when I gave them a taste! (were, is)

8. We _____ tomatoes over the summer. (grew, growed)

Conquer Grammar • Grade 3 • © Newmark Learning, LLC

Name _____ Date _____

Irregular Past Tense Verbs

Past tense verbs tell about actions that already happened. Past tense verbs that do not end in **-ed** are irregular. Some examples of verbs and their irregular past tense forms include **keep/kept**, **find/found**, **buy/bought**, and **make/made**.

Write the past tense form of the verb in the parentheses ( ).

1. I _____ two inches in the last year. (grow)

2. I _____ that most of my clothes were too small. (find)

3. My dad _____ me some new clothes at the mall. (buy)

4. The bright colors _____ me happy! (make)

5. I _____ my new sandals yesterday. (wear)

6. It _____ so hot outside! (to be)

7. My sandals _____ my feet cool. (keep)

Name _____ Date _____

Irregular Past Tense Verbs

> Past tense verbs tell about actions that already happened. Past tense verbs that do not end in **-d** or **-ed** are irregular. Some examples of verbs and their irregular past tense forms include **find/found, grow/grew, buy/bought, get/got,** and **make/made**.

Write the correct form of the verb in the parentheses ( ) to complete each sentence.

1. We _____ a foot of snow on the first day of spring last year. (get)

2. My dad woke me up late because I _____ no school. (have)

3. Austin and I _____ a snow fort in the front yard. (make)

4. We _____ tree branches to use as flags for the fort. (find)

5. The tree branches _____ already on the ground. (to be)

6. That spring, the flowers _____ right through the snow! (grow)

7. It was lucky that we _____ a new shovel. (buy)

8. Today is the first day of spring, and it _____ warm and sunny. (to be)

Conquer Grammar • Grade 3 • © Newmark Learning, LLC

Name _____   Date _____

Irregular Past Tense Verbs

Past tense verbs tell about actions that already happened. Past tense verbs that do not end in **-ed** are irregular. Some examples of verbs and their irregular past tense forms include:

Present Tense	Irregular Past Tense
grow	grew
make	made
find	found
get	got
buy	bought

Choose the correct verb from the box to complete each sentence. Write it on the line.

grow	make	grew	made	found
find	get	buy	got	bought

1. Tina _____ four inches in the last year.

2. Stephen and Alex _____ dinner for their grandma.

3. I _____ my cousin a gift with the money I saved.

4. I misplaced your ball and have not _____ it yet.

5. I _____ a chill after I went out without a coat.

6. Who _____ these lovely flowers?

7. I need to _____ my notebook.

Name _____   Date _____

Irregular Past Tense Verbs

> Past tense verbs tell about actions that already happened.
> Past tense verbs that do not end in **-ed** are irregular.

Choose the correct verb from the box to complete each sentence. Write it on the line.

am	was	were	make
made	grew	found	had

1. I _____ a kickball game last Sunday.

2. My dad _____ the team's uniforms.

3. Tito _____ the catcher last year.

4. This year, I _____ pitching.

5. The ball got lost, but then the coach _____ it.

Rewrite each sentence with the past tense form of the underlined verb.

6. When she had a garden, my aunt <u>grows</u> different vegetables.

_____

7. The ice cream store <u>makes</u> many types of flavors.

_____

Conquer Grammar • Grade 3 • © Newmark Learning, LLC

Name _____ Date _____

Irregular and Regular Past Tense Verbs

> Past tense verbs tell about actions that already happened. Past tense verbs that do not end in **-d** or **-ed** are irregular. Some examples of verbs and their irregular past tense forms include **have/had**, **grow/grew**, **find/found**, and **make/made**.

Rewrite each sentence. Replace the underlined verb with the past tense form. There is a mix of regular and irregular verbs.

1. We <u>will have</u> our first soccer game on Saturday.

   _____

2. We <u>are</u> in first place in the league.

   _____

3. I <u>am</u> the goalie and team captain.

   _____

4. Maria <u>makes</u> all her penalty shots.

   _____

5. Maria <u>hopes</u> to be the team captain.

   _____

6. She <u>will grow</u> three inches taller this year!

   _____

7. Maria and I <u>find</u> that being tall helps to block goals.

   _____

Name _____   Date _____

Irregular Verbs: *to be* and *have*

Past tense verbs that do not end in **-ed** are irregular. **To be** and **have** are examples of verbs with irregular past tense and plural forms.

to be

Singular	Present	Past
I	am	was
you	are	were
he/she/it	is	was

Plural		
we	are	were
they	are	were

have

Singular	Present	Past
I	have	had
you	have	had
he/she/it	has	had

Plural		
we	have	had
they	have	had

Circle the correct verb in the parentheses ( ).
Write the complete sentence on the line.

1. David (is   are) coming over today.

   _____

2. I (am   was) getting some snacks ready now.

   _____

3. Jamal and Kendra (was   were) here yesterday.

   _____

4. They (have   had) a lot of fun!

   _____

Name _____ Date _____

Subject-Verb Agreement

> The subject of a sentence is a noun that tells whom or what the sentence is about. The verb tells what the subject does. The subject and the verb in a sentence must agree. A singular subject takes a singular verb. A plural subject takes a plural verb. Most singular verbs end in **s**. Removing the final **s** from the verbs makes the verbs plural.
> **Singular Subject:** Those <u>boys</u> **play** baseball.
> **Plural Subject:** That <u>girl</u> **plays** tennis.

Determine whether the subject of each sentence is singular or plural. Circle the correct verb. Then write it on the line.

1. Anthony _____ the bowls on the top shelf.

   (place, places)

2. Mia _____ the flute, and she is very talented.

   (play, plays)

3. My cousins _____ in the chorus.

   (sing, sings)

4. Trevon _____ many science books.

   (read, reads)

5. The flowers _____ so sweet!

   (smell, smells)

Name _____   Date _____

Subject-Verb Agreement

> The subject of a sentence is a noun that tells whom or what the sentence is about. The verb tells what the subject does. The subject and the verb in a sentence must agree. A singular subject takes a singular verb. A plural subject takes a plural verb. Most singular verbs end in **s**. Removing the final **s** makes the verbs plural.
>
> **Singular Subject:** <u>Katie</u> **loves** her brothers very much.
> **Plural Subject:** <u>Fred and Tito</u> **love** their sister, too.

Determine whether the subject of each sentence is singular or plural. Circle the correct verb. Then write the complete sentence on the line.

1. Marisol (practice, practices) the piano every day.

   _____

2. All the students (takes, take) the subway to the museum.

   _____

3. We (recycle, recycles) paper and plastic at school.

   _____

4. Both of my cats (hide, hides) under my bed.

   _____

5. He (hear, hears) you talking from across the room.

   _____

Conquer Grammar • Grade 3 • © Newmark Learning, LLC

Name _____   Date _____

Subject-Verb Agreement

> The subject of a sentence is a noun that tells whom or what the sentence is about. The verb tells what the subject does. The subject and the verb in a sentence must agree. A singular subject takes a singular verb. A plural subject takes a plural verb. Most singular verbs end in **s**. Removing the final **s** from the verbs makes the verbs plural.
> **Singular Subject:** <u>Charlie</u> **enjoys** going to the beach.
> **Plural Subject:** <u>Alexi and Moira</u> **enjoy** the ocean.

Determine whether the subject of each sentence is singular or plural. Circle the correct verb. Then write the complete sentence on the line.

1. Mr. Torres (coach, coaches) our baseball team.

   _____

2. Jordan (use, uses) a list to shop for groceries.

   _____

3. Our parents (drive, drives) very carefully.

   _____

4. The twins both (play, plays) musical instruments.

   _____

5. When I can't reach the top shelf, I (ask, asks) for help.

   _____

Name _____ Date _____

Subject-Verb Agreement

The subject of a sentence is a noun that tells whom or what the sentence is about. The verb tells what the subject does. The subject and the verb in a sentence must agree. A singular subject takes a singular verb. A plural subject takes a plural verb. Most singular verbs end in **s**. Removing the final **s** from the verbs makes the verbs plural.

Singular Subject: The meal **is** spicy.

Plural Subject: My brothers **are** very kind.

Rewrite each sentence with the correct subject-verb agreement.

1. Ella water the flowers in her garden.

   _____

2. Gino and Mary works in the same office.

   _____

3. My cousin walk his new dog.

   _____

4. My mom and dad wants to take the family on vacation.

   _____

5. When it's sunny outside, I rides my bicycle.

   _____

Name _____ Date _____

Subject and Object Pronouns

A pronoun takes the place of a subject or object in a sentence. **I**, **you**, **he**, **she**, **it**, **we**, and **they** are subject pronouns. Use a subject pronoun when a pronoun is the subject of a sentence (**me** and **you** can be both object and subject pronouns). **Me**, **you**, **him**, **her**, **it**, **us**, and **them** are object pronouns. You and it can be both Use an object pronoun when a pronoun is the object of a verb or a preposition.

Subject Pronoun: Ricky went outside. **He** took a walk.
Object Pronoun: Ariel saw Mr. Miller. She waved to **him**.

Underline the subject of the first sentence. Circle the pronoun in the second sentence that replaces it.

1. The principal walked down the hallway. She greeted every student by name.

2. Michael and Jason studied together. They both got a good score on this test.

3. Saturday, Jenna went to a party. She had a wonderful time.

4. This summer, the local pool will reopen. It will be a good place to keep cool.

Circle the object of the first sentence. Underline the pronoun in the second sentence that replaces it.

5. Mom invited our cousins to spend the weekend. My brother took them swimming.

6. Jack and Abby happily joined my brother. Both cousins like him a lot.

7. The lifeguard blew a whistle. The swimmers heard it and left the pool.

Name _____ Date _____

Pronoun-Antecedent Agreement

> The noun that a pronoun replaces is called an antecedent. A pronoun and its antecedent must match in number and person. In the example below, **Maria**, **her**, and **she** match because they all refer to one girl.
>
> **Maria** lost **her** scarf, but **she** found it at the end of the day.

Circle the correct pronoun and write it on the line. Then underline the antecedent.

1. Lorenzo went to see _____ math tutor after school.

    her   his   their

2. The boys will play _____ first game on Sunday.

    its   his   their

3. Will you please wash the dishes and put _____ away?

    our   them   her

4. I will do my homework now and hand _____ in tomorrow.

    it   he   them

5. Marco is leaving soon. I will really miss _____.

    him   her   them

6. Sue, please put _____ shoes away so I don't trip on them!

    me   you   your

Conquer Grammar • Grade 3 • © Newmark Learning, LLC

37

Name _____ Date _____

Pronoun-Antecedent Agreement

> The noun that a pronoun replaces is called an antecedent. A pronoun and its antecedent must match in number and person. In the example below, **Sergio**, **his**, and **he** match because they all refer to one boy.
>
> **Sergio** went to **his** class, and **he** sat in **his** seat.

Choose the correct pronoun from the box to complete each sentence. Write it on the line. Make sure the pronoun and its antecendent agree.

you	your	he	him	she
her	they	their	we	our

1. Troy, will _____ please stop bothering me?

2. Arjun and Ahmed are going to help _____ dad rake.

3. I will take care of my brother when _____ wakes up.

4. Andy and I are best friends, so _____ do everything together.

5. I tried to call Marco, but I can't reach _____.

6. Natalie, is this _____ backpack?

Name _____ Date _____

Possessive Pronouns

A possessive pronoun shows who or what owns something. **My**, **mine**, **your**, **yours**, **her**, **hers**, **his**, **its**, **our**, **ours**, **their**, and **theirs** are possessive pronouns. A possessive pronoun never has an apostrophe.

This is not **my** binder. That red one is **mine**.
This sweater is **hers**. I will take it to **her** house tomorrow.

Circle the possessive pronoun that correctly completes each sentence.

1. Kayla opened (its, her) bedroom window.

2. The excited dog wagged (its, their) tail.

3. The students rode (their, theirs) skateboards after school.

4. Lilly, is this pencil (your, yours)?

5. I finished every book on (my, mine) summer reading list.

6. (Our, Ours) aunt always makes me laugh.

7. (Their, Mine) cat is the friendliest cat I know.

8. Sam, I found (yours, your) coat!

Name _____ Date _____

Indefinite Pronouns

> Indefinite pronouns take the place of a noun or noun phrase in a sentence. Indefinite pronouns do not refer to specific people, places, or things. Some examples of indefinite pronouns include **everyone**, **everything**, **anyone**, **anywhere**, **anything**, **someone**, **somewhere**, **something**, **no one**, **nowhere**, **nothing**.

Choose the correct pronoun in the parentheses ( ) to complete each sentence. Write the sentence on the line.

1. My kind mother will help (anyone, no one) who is deserving.

   _____

2. There is (anyone, no one) kinder than my mother.

   _____

3. Because we love the beach, we will go (somewhere, nowhere) near an ocean.

   _____

   _____

4. (Anyone, Everyone) was happy to see the clouds parting.

   _____

5. (Nothing, Everything) makes me laugh more than a funny movie.

   _____

Name _____ Date _____

Reflexive Pronouns

Reflexive pronouns refer back to the subject of a sentence and always end in **-self** or **-selves**. **Myself**, **yourself**, **himself**, **herself**, **itself**, **ourselves**, **yourselves**, and **themselves** are reflexive pronouns.

I bought **myself** a toy.

Write a reflexive pronoun to complete each sentence.

1. I bought _____ a comic book.

2. They baked those cookies _____.

3. Joshua poured _____ a glass of water.

4. Malina built the dresser _____.

5. The friends asked _____ if they should see the scary movie or the comedy.

6. Jake and I made _____ a tasty dinner.

7. The cat cleaned _____ after it came in from the rain.

8. You can solve the math problem _____.

Name _____ Date _____

Reciprocal Pronouns

> Use the reciprocal pronoun **each other** to refer to two people or things performing the same action toward each other. Use the reciprocal pronoun **one another** to refer to three or more people or things performing the same action toward one another.
>
> Joe and Mario were happy to see **each other**.
> We and all the visitors greeted **one another.**

Write the reciprocal pronoun that correctly completes the sentence: *each other* **or** *one another*.

1. My brother and my father look just like _____.

2. All the people in the crowded subway were bumping against _____.

3. When you meet a new teammate, you should tell _____ your names.

4. Can we all agree to get along with _____?

5. The team members shook hands with _____ after the game.

6. I cannot believe it has been one whole year since you and I have seen _____.

Name _____ Date _____

Reciprocal Pronouns

> Reciprocal pronouns help eliminate repetitive sentences or repetition within a sentence. Use the reciprocal pronoun **each other** to show that two people or things are performing the same action toward each other. Use the reciprocal pronoun **one another** to refer to three or more people or things perfomring the same action toward one another.
>
> They looked at **each other**.
> The teachers and students respect **one another**.

Rewrite the sentence or sentences using *each other* **or** *one another.*

1. Brad will meet Yolanda at the movies. Yolanda will meet Brad at the movies.

   _____

2. My dog loves my cat, and my cat loves my dog.

   _____

3. All the children stared at the owls, and all the owls stared at the children.

   _____

4. Matt passed the ball to Kit. Kit passed the ball to Matt.

   _____

5. The members of the team thanked the fans, and the fans thanked the members of the team.

   _____

Name _____ Date _____

Reciprocal Pronouns

> Use a reciprocal pronoun when two or more people or things are performing the same action and are both affected by the action in the same way. Use **each other** to refer to two people or things. Use **One another** to refer to three or more people or things.
>
> Bella and Drew smiled at **each other.**
> After the game, all the players high-fived **one another.**

Rewrite each sentence with the reciprocal pronoun *each other* or *one another*.

1. Abby admired Manny, and Manny admired Abby.

   _____

2. Each musician complimented all the other musicians.

   _____

3. My dad usually agrees with my mom, and my mom usually agrees with my dad.

   _____

4. My cat gets along with my two dogs. My two dogs get along with my cat.

   _____

5. Tanya took turns writing to Noel. Noel took turns writing to Tanya.

   _____

Name _____ Date _____

Adjectives

> Adjectives are words that describe nouns. An adjective may express an opinion or describe the look or feel of the noun, its age, color, origin, or the material it is made of.
>
> **Opinion:** a **tasty** meal   **Look or feel:** a **kind** friend
> **Age:** an **old** piano   **Color:** a **red** apple
> **Origin:** an **Australian** flag **Material:** a **cotton** shirt
> **Size:** a **big** house   **Shape:** a **round** clock

Circle the adjective in each sentence. Underline the noun it describes.

1. The tiny puppy had a lot of energy.

2. Sara sat on the comfortable chair.

3. The brown branches and the green leaves of the tree shaded us from the sun.

4. We found a ladybug on the wooden fence.

Complete each sentence. Write an adjective that matches the category in the parentheses ( ).

5. This _____ sweater is my favorite.   (color)

6. Pages from the _____ book fell out.   (age)

7. We ate _____ food at the party.   (opinion)

Conquer Grammar • Grade 3 • © Newmark Learning, LLC

Name _____ Date _____

Adjectives

> Adjectives are words that describe nouns. An adjective may express an opinion or describe the look or feel of the noun, its age, color, origin, or the material it is made of.
>
> **Opinion:** a **fancy** house **Look or feel:** a **shiny** apple
> **Age:** an **eight-year-old** girl **Color:** a **yellow** lemon
> **Origin:** an **American** flag **Material:** a **metal** shelf
> **Size:** a **small** cat **Shape:** a **square** table

Circle the adjective in each sentence. Underline the noun it describes.

1. This newborn baby is my sister.

2. The family went to an Italian restaurant.

3. Artistic students entered their work in the competition.

4. We shopped for groceries at a local store.

Complete each sentence. Write an adjective that matches the category in the parentheses ( ).

5. He sat on the _____ rug in the living room. (look/feel)

6. I must return this _____ book to the library. (opinion)

7. The _____ house was beautiful. (material)

46   Conquer Grammar • Grade 3 • © Newmark Learning, LLC

Name _____ Date _____

Adverbs

> Adverbs give more information about where or when an action occurs or how it happens. An adverb can appear before or after the verb it modifies or in between different verb parts.
> **Where:** The wind was <u>blowing</u> **everywhere**.
> **When: Later,** we will <u>watch</u> a movie.
> **How:** The children were <u>laughing</u> **loudly**.

Circle the adverb in each sentence. Then write if it shows *where*, *when*, or *how* the action happens.

1. My little brother splashed happily in the wading pool. _____

2. We sat comfortably on the soft cushions. _____

3. I walk my dog daily. _____

4. Our volleyball team practices indoors. _____

5. I will celebrate my birthday soon. _____

6. The detective cleverly solved the case. _____

7. The music classroom is upstairs. _____

8. Yesterday, I bought a new shirt. _____

Name _____ Date _____

Adverbs

> Adverbs give more information about where or when an action occurs or how it happens. An adverb can appear before or after the verb it modifies or in between different verb parts. Adverbs can also modify an adjective or another adverb. In those cases, the adverb should appear before the word it modifies.
> **Modifies a verb:** The rain <u>fell</u> **gently**.
> **Modifies an adjective:** This is a **slightly** <u>spicy</u> dinner.
> **Modifies another adverb:** Our turtle moves **very** <u>slowly</u>.

Circle the adverb in each sentence. Underline the word it describes.

1. Our teacher thought we would do quite well on the test.

2. She ran quickly down the soccer field.

3. These are incredibly fluffy blankets.

4. Chris climbed the tree skillfully.

Complete each sentence. Write an adjective that matches the category in the parentheses ( ).

5. We like to play _____. (where)

6. I _____ walk the dog with my brother. (when)

7. This jacket fits _____. (how)

48   Conquer Grammar • Grade 3 • © Newmark Learning, LLC

Name _____ Date _____

Adjectives and Adverbs

> Adjectives describe, or tell more about, nouns.
>
> Sasha is a **thoughtful** friend. He sent Reba a **dozen yellow** daisies.
>
> Adverbs describe or tell more about verbs, adjectives, and other adverbs.
>
> The bus drove **very slowly** up the street. Then it stopped **completely**.

Circle whether the word in dark type is an adjective or an adverb. Then underline the word it describes.

1. Yesterday at school, the track team had an **important** race.

   adjective   adverb

2. Jenna sprinted **away** from the starting point.

   adjective   adverb

3. In the beginning of the race, she held an **enormous** lead.

   adjective   adverb

4. We all **mistakenly** believed that she would win.

   adjective   adverb

5. However, she **quickly** fell behind the other runners.

   adjective   adverb

Adjectives and Adverbs

Adjectives describe, or tell more about, nouns. Some examples of adjectives include **green**, **tall**, **scared**, **wealthy**, **sour**, and **intelligent**. Adverbs describe, or tell more about, verbs, adjectives, and other adverbs. Some examples of adverbs include **honestly**, **foolishly**, **kindly**, **usually**, **very**, **down**, and **up**.

Circle the adjective in each sentence. Underline the word it describes.

1. We approached the scariest house I have ever seen.

2. Melvin walked up the crumbling steps.

3. He knocked on the ancient door.

4. "Who's there?" called out a spooky voice.

Circle the adverb in each sentence. Underline the word it describes.

5. Melvin gasped loudly.

6. He ran quickly down the steps, with fear on his face.

7. Melvin's adventure ended badly!

Name _____ Date _____

Adjectives and Adverbs

> Adjectives describe, or tell more about, nouns and pronouns. Some examples of adjectives include **three, pleasant, windy, harmful,** and **amazing**. Adverbs describe or tell more about verbs, adjectives, and other adverbs. Some examples of adverbs include **cheerfully, carefully, often, soon**, and **very**.

Circle the adjective in each sentence. Underline the word it describes.

1. Max's mother gave him a long list of things she needed.

2. Shopping was one of Max's favorite activities.

3. He loved picking out the reddest berries.

4. He enjoyed choosing nutritious vegetables.

Circle the adverb in each sentence. Underline the word it describes.

5. Max walked quickly through the store.

6. He wanted time to easily buy everything on the list!

7. Max's mother trusts him completely to do the grocery shopping.

8. Max is a very responsible boy!

Name _____ Date _____

Comparatives

> Comparative adjectives and adverbs compare two people, places, or things. Follow these spelling rules to form comparative adjectives or adverbs: Add **-er** to the end of the adjective or adverb: **taller**. If the word ends in **-y**, change the **y** to **i** and then add **-er**: **prettier**. If the word ends in **-e**, just add **-r**: **later**. If the word ends in a single vowel and a consonant, double the consonant and add **-er**: **bigger**.
> For longer adjectives or adverbs, add the word **more** in front of the adjective or adverb: **more interesting**.

Write the comparative form of the underlined adjective or adverb. You may need to change the spelling of the word.

1. Gabby and Eve are hard workers, but Eve works _____.

2. This spring is rainy, but last spring was _____.

3. Justine likes sweet apples. Which one is _____ —the green or the red?

4. My dog is big, but my neighbor's dog is even _____.

5. This winter is cold, but last winter was _____.

6. I knew the movie would be funny, but it was _____ than I expected!

7. The last soccer coach was strict, but this one is even _____.

52   Conquer Grammar • Grade 3 • © Newmark Learning, LLC

Name _____ Date _____

Superlatives

> Superlative adjectives or adverbs compare three or more people, places, or things. Follow these spelling rules to form superlative adjectives or adverbs: Add **-est** to the end of the adjective or adverb: **tallest**. If the word ends in **-y**, change the **y** to **i** and then add **-est**: **prettiest**. If the word ends in **-e**, just add **-st**: **latest**. If the word ends in a single vowel and a consonant, double the consonant and add **-est**: **biggest**.
> For longer adjectives or adverbs, add the word **most** in front of the adjective or adverb: **most interesting**.

Write the superlative form of the underlined adjective or adverb. You may need to change the spelling of the word.

1. I have heard many <u>noisy</u> birds, but this one is the _____.

2. Mom wants a <u>big</u> pumpkin. She asked me to get the _____ one I could find.

3. I like <u>hot</u> peppers! Which of these is the _____?

4. That tree is <u>tall</u>. It is the _____ tree I have ever seen.

5. You were so <u>brave</u>! That was the _____ thing you have done.

6. Of all the <u>sad</u> movies I have seen, this one is the _____.

7. The puppies are so <u>little</u>. I want the _____ one!

Name _____ Date _____

Comparatives and Superlatives

> Comparative adjectives and adverbs compare two people, places, or things. Superlative adjectives or adverbs compare three or more people, places, or things. Follow these rules to form comparatives and superlatives:
>
> 1. Add **-er** or **-est** to the end of the adjective or adverb.
>
> | | **Comparative** | **Superlative** |
> |---|---|---|
> | small | smaller | smallest |
>
> 2. For longer adjectives or adverbs, add the word **more** or **most** in front of the adjective or adverb.
>
> | | **Comparative** | **Superlative** |
> |---|---|---|
> | artistic | more artistic | most artistic |
>
> 3. Some comparatives and superlatives are irregular and do not follow a pattern. For example:
>
> | | **Comparative** | **Superlative** |
> |---|---|---|
> | good | better | best |

Write the comparative form of the underlined adjective or adverb.

1. This kitten is <u>adorable</u>, but the black one is _____.

2. This sweater is <u>cozy</u>, but that blanket is even _____.

3. I enjoy a <u>good</u> puzzle. Which of these two is _____.

Write the superlative form of the underlined adjective or adverb.

4. Bike trails can be <u>dangerous</u>. Which one is the _____.

5. I am so <u>happy</u>! This is the _____ I've ever been!

6. This bowl is <u>large</u>, but that bowl is the _____ I have ever seen!

Name _____ Date _____

Comparatives and Superlatives

> Follow these rules to form comparative and superlative adjectives and adverbs:
>
> 1. Add **-er** or **-est** to the end of the adjective or adverb.
>
> | | **Comparative** | **Superlative** |
> |----------|-----------------|-----------------|
> | wise | wiser | wisest |
>
> 2. For longer adjectives or adverbs, add the word **more** or **most** in front of the adjective or adverb.
>
> | | **Comparative** | **Superlative** |
> |-----------|------------------|------------------|
> | carefully | more carefully | most carefully |
>
> 3. Some comparatives and superlatives are irregular and do not follow a pattern. For example:
>
> | | **Comparative** | **Superlative** |
> |-----|-----------------|-----------------|
> | bad | worse | worst |

Circle the comparative or superlative that correctly completes each sentence. Write it on the line.

1. Yesterday, I saw the _____ movie I have ever seen!
   most bad   worst

2. Which are the _____—the apples, the oranges, or the blueberries?   most delicious   more delicious

3. The mayor is the _____ official in city government.
   more important   most important

4. I am much _____ at basketball than bowling.
   better   best

5. My green shirt is _____ than my white one.
   most colorful   more colorful

Name _____ Date _____

Comparatives and Superlatives

> Follow these rules to form comparative and superlative adjectives and adverbs:
> 1. Add **-er** or **-est** to the end of the adjective or adverb.
>
> | | **Comparative** | **Superlative** |
> |---|---|---|
> | short | shorter | shortest |
>
> 2. For longer adjectives or adverbs, add the word **more** or **most** in front of the adjective or adverb.
>
> | | **Comparative** | **Superlative** |
> |---|---|---|
> | comfortable | more comfortable | most comfortable |
>
> 3. Some comparatives and superlatives are irregular and do not follow a pattern. For example:
>
> | | **Comparative** | **Superlative** |
> |---|---|---|
> | bad | worse | worst |

Write the comparative or superlative of the word in the parentheses ( ). You may need to change the spelling of the word.

1. There are so many choices! Which kind of yogurt do you like _____? (good)

2. I like both vanilla and blueberry yogurt, but I like vanilla _____. (good)

3. I think this striped sweater is _____ than the plaid one. (attractive)

4. That's the _____ scarf in the store! (ugly)

5. Ms. Juarez is the _____ teacher in my school. (popular)

56   Conquer Grammar • Grade 3 • © Newmark Learning, LLC

Name _____ Date _____

Comparatives and Superlatives

Follow these rules to form comparative and superlative adjectives and adverbs:

1. Add **-er** or **-est** to the end of the adjective or adverb.
            Comparative   **Superlative**
   healthy   healthier   healthiest

2. For longer adjectives or adverbs, add the word **more** or **most** in front of the adjective or adverb.
            Comparative   **Superlative**
   generous   more generous   most generous

3. Some comparatives and superlatives are irregular and do not follow a pattern. For example:
            Comparative   **Superlative**
   good   better   best

Write the comparative or superlative of the word in the parentheses ( ). You may need to change the spelling of the word.

1. Which of these two pictures did you like _____? (good)

2. That is the _____ pony I have ever seen! (tiny)

3. The yellow chair is much _____ than the blue one. (comfortable)

4. That's the _____ I've ever done on a test! (good)

5. My uncle Roberto is the _____ person I know. (wise)

6. I'm _____ in age to my older sister than to my younger one. (close)

7. This is the _____ food I've ever tasted! (disgusting)

Conquer Grammar • Grade 3 • © Newmark Learning, LLC   57

Name _____ Date _____

Comparatives and Superlatives

> Follow these rules to form comparative and superlative adjectives and adverbs:
> 1. Add **-er** or **-est** to the end of the adjective or adverb.
>
> | | **Comparative** | **Superlative** |
> |---|---|---|
> | funny | funnier | funniest |
>
> 2. For longer adjectives or adverbs, add the word **more** or **most** in front of the adjective or adverb.
>
> | | **Comparative** | **Superlative** |
> |---|---|---|
> | careful | more careful | most careful |
>
> 3. Some comparatives and superlatives are irregular and do not follow a pattern. For example:
>
> | | **Comparative** | **Superlative** |
> |---|---|---|
> | good | better | best |

Circle the incorrect word in each sentence. Write the correct comparative or superlative on the line.

1. I think your explanation is confusinger than mine.
   _____

2. These are the beautifulest paintings in the art gallery.
   _____

3. Which yogurt do you think is gooder—blueberry or coffee?
   _____

4. A storm on field day? This is the baddest day ever! _____

5. Who is your goodest friend on the team? _____

6. I'm embarrasseder now than I was before.
   _____

Name _____ Date _____

Prepositions

> A prepositional phrase is a group of words that usually includes a preposition and a noun or pronoun along with any modifiers. Prepositional phrases often answer questions such as **which one? where? when? how? how long?**
>
> **Which one?** The boy **in** the blue sweater is my brother.
> **Where?** The red pencil is **in** the desk drawer.
> **When?** I will see you **after** recess.
> **How?** She went into the dark cave, **with** all her courage.
> **How long?** The man was lost in the woods **for** two days.

Write a preposition to begin the prepositional phrase that answers the question in the parentheses ( ).

1. _____ dinner, Edgar washed the dishes.
   (When?)

2. The magazine _____ the shiny cover belongs to me.
   (Which one?)

3. It has been raining _____ several hours.
   (How long?)

4. Peter knocked over the vase _____ his backpack.
   (How?)

5. I always put my bike away _____ the garage.
   (Where?)

6. The girl _____ the red dress is my sister.
   (Which one?)

Conquer Grammar • Grade 3 • © Newmark Learning, LLC   59

Name _____ Date _____

Prepositions

> A prepositional phrase is a group of words that usually includes a preposition and a noun or pronoun along with any modifiers. Only object pronouns can be used in prepositional phrases.
> **Incorrect:** Sean practiced soccer kicks with **I**.
> **Correct:** Sean practiced soccer kicks with **me**.
>
> **Incorrect:** Sean practiced soccer kicks with Crystal and **I**.
> **Correct:** Sean practiced soccer kicks with **Crystal** and **me**.
> Sean practiced soccer kicks with **her** and **me**.

Underline the preposition in each sentence. Then circle the correct pronoun or pronouns in the parentheses ( ).

1. Laurel threw the ball between Macy and (I, me).

2. Then I threw the ball toward (she, her).

3. In the first thirty minutes, no one scored a run except Macy, Laurel, and (I, me).

4. Did your mom wave to (he, him) and (they, them)?

5. Yes, and my whole family cheered for (we, us).

6. Macy likes playing soccer on the same team with Laurel and (I, me).

7. After the game, I had ice cream with (she, her).

Name _____ Date _____

Prepositions

> A prepositional phrase is a group of words that usually includes a preposition and a noun or pronoun along with any modifiers. Prepositional phrases often answer questions such as **which one? where? when? how? how long?**
>
> **Which one?** Minna broke the cup **with** the blue handle.
> **Where?** Put your book **on** the shelf.
> **When?** My grandmother will visit **in** the summer.
> **How?** Our teacher spoke **with** great excitement.
> **How long?** I walked **for** an hour.

Underline the preposition in each sentence. Then circle the word in the parentheses ( ) that tells which question the prepositional phrase answers.

1. Regina raked all the leaves in the yard.
   where   how

2. My sister planted tulips behind our house.
   which one   where

3. I hope I can go swimming during my vacation.
   how long   when

4. Natalie was wearing a jacket with blue stripes.
   when   which one

5. Eduardo went camping for the weekend.
   which one   how long

6. Can you bring me the book on the desk?
   how long   where

Name _____ Date _____

Conjunctions

> Use a comma and a conjunction such as **and**, **or**, **but**, and **so** to combine two sentences to form a compound sentence. Place the comma before the conjunction.
>   Byron played baseball. Jerry played soccer.
>   Byron played baseball, **and** Jerry played soccer.

Combine each pair of sentences to form one compound sentence. Use a comma and the conjunction in the parentheses ( ). Write the sentence on the line.

1. I like yogurt. I eat it often. (so)

   _____

2. Jake and Tommy are friends. They are in the same class. (and)

   _____

3. Angela likes roller coasters. I prefer Ferris wheels. (but)

   _____

4. Lilly can bike near the beach. She can bike in the park. (or)

   _____

5. Mr. Dibo coaches the football team. He conducts the choir. (and)

   _____

   _____

6. I can meet you on Saturday. Sunday would be a better day. (but)

   _____

   _____

Name _____   Date _____

Commas for Greetings and Closings

Letters or e-mails begin with a greeting and end with a closing. A greeting consists of a word such as **Dear** or **Hi** and the name of the person you are writing to, followed by a comma. Every word in a greeting should begin with a capital letter.

Dear Mrs. Bryant,   **Hi** Carmelo,   **Hello,** James,

A closing consists of a word or words such as **Yours**, **Yours truly**, **Love**, or **Sincerely** followed by a comma, and the author's name on the next line. Only the first word in a closing should begin with a capital letter.

Yours,   **Lots of love,**   **Sincerely,**
Michelle   Mom   Ms. Marlon

Circle whether each group of words is a greeting or a closing. Then rewrite it correctly on the lines.

1. Hello Emily   greeting   closing   _____

2. Fondly Sam   greeting   closing   _____

3. Dear Grandma   greeting   closing   _____

4. Your pal Dan   greeting   closing   _____

5. Sincerely Pam   greeting   closing   _____

Conquer Grammar • Grade 3 • © Newmark Learning, LLC

Name _____ Date _____

End Marks

> An end mark is the punctuation that comes at the end of a sentence.
>
> Statements, or telling sentences, end in a period: **.**
>
> Sentences that ask a question end in a question mark: **?**
>
> Sentences that show strong feeling end in an exclamation mark: **!**
>
> Riley is reading a book**.**
> What is the name of the book**?**
> I love that book**!**

Read each sentence. Write the correct end mark.

1. What flavor of ice cream is your favorite ____

2. I just finished reading a book about dolphins ____

3. That was the funniest joke I have ever heard ____

4. When will dinner be ready ____

5. Dinner will be ready at six o'clock ____

6. I'll set the table tonight ____

7. That bird just caught a fish ____

8. Do you have time to go to the store ____

Name _____ Date _____

End Marks

> An end mark is the punctuation that comes at the end of a sentence.
> Statements, or telling sentences, end in a period: **.**
> Sentences that ask a question end in a question mark: **?**
> Sentences that show strong feeling end in an exclamation mark: **!**

Rewrite each sentence with the correct end mark.

1. I'm going to be very late if I don't hurry

   _____

2. Did you see the full moon last night

   _____

3. How many people will be here for dinner

   _____

4. I will write my book report on Tuesday.

   _____

5. We're getting a puppy today

   _____

6. Are you ready to perform in the play tonight

   _____

7. Yes, and I am very excited

   _____

Name _____ Date _____

Contractions

> Some contractions consist of a pronoun and a verb combined into a single word. An apostrophe (') replaces the dropped letter or letters in a contraction.
>
> | Pronoun and Verb | Contraction |
> |---|---|
> | I am | I'm |
> | He is, She is, It is | He's, She's, It's |
> | We are | We're |
> | You are | You're |
> | They are | They're |

Write the contraction of the words in the parentheses ( ).

1. Mrs. Murphy asked if _____ staying for lunch. (you are)

2. _____ making hamburgers and potato salad. (She is)

3. Tomorrow, _____ supposed to rain all day. (it is)

4. Our cat is sick so _____ bringing her to the vet. (we are)

5. _____ always on time for school. (I am)

6. The choir needs more singers, so _____ going to audition. (he is)

Name _____   Date _____

Contractions

> Some contractions consist of a pronoun and a verb combined into a single word. An apostrophe (') replaces the dropped letter or letters in a contraction.
>
> | Pronoun and Verb | Contractions |
> |---|---|
> | I will | I'll |
> | He will, She will, It will | He'll, She'll, It'll |
> | We will | We'll |
> | You will | You'll |
> | They will | They'll |

Rewrite each sentence. Replace the underlined words with a contraction.

1. <u>We will</u> meet you at the airport.

   _____

2. Please tell me what time <u>you will</u> be here.

   _____

3. <u>I will</u> see you when you arrive.

   _____

4. <u>It will</u> be wonderful to spend time together.

   _____

5. If it rains, <u>they will</u> bring an umbrella.

Punctuate Dialogue

Dialogue is a conversation between two or more characters. Quotation marks show the exact words a speaker says.
Use a comma to separate the speaker's introduction or tag from the words he or she says. Place periods inside quotation marks. If the dialogue itself ends in a question mark or an exclamation point, place the punctuation inside the final quotation mark and drop the comma.

Tara said, "We must all have positive attitudes."
"We must all have positive attitudes," **said Tara**.

Rewrite each sentence, with correct punctuation.

1. Monique said I will start my homework after dinner.

2. I hope you won't stay up too late said Mom.

3. I have a lot of homework replied Monique. I'll start now.

4. Dad said I'll call you when dinner is ready.

5. Thanks, Dad said Monique.

6. Dad called Monique! Don't forget your books!

Punctuate Dialogue

> Dialogue is a conversation between two or more characters. Quotation marks show the exact words a speaker says.
> Use a comma to separate the speaker's introduction or tag from the words he or she says. Place periods inside quotation marks. If the dialogue itself ends in a question mark or an exclamation point, place the punctuation inside the final quotation mark and drop the comma.
>
> **Alicia said,** "We should all try to get along."
>
> "We should all try to get along," **said Alicia.**

Rewrite each sentence with correct punctuation.

1. Cammy said Let's meet at the library after school.

2. I can be there at four o'clock answered Jake.

3. Tammy said I'm right here behind you.

4. Tom exclaimed I can't believe that you didn't call me!

5. Molly replied I was so busy last night that I forgot.

6. I'm sorry added Molly. I won't forget again.

Name _____ Date _____

Punctuate Dialogue

Dialogue is a conversation between two or more characters. Quotation marks show the exact words a speaker says. Use a comma to separate the speaker's introduction or tag from the words he or she says. Place periods inside quotation marks. If the dialogue itself ends in a question mark or an exclamation point, place the punctuation inside the final quotation mark and drop the comma.

Coach Jones said, "You are late."
"Why are you late again**?**" **asked Coach Jones**.
"I'm really sorry," apologized Frances**.** "I missed the bus**.**"

Rewrite each sentence with correct punctuation.

1. Can you help me make dinner? Sandeep asked.

   _____

2. Yes, I can help you Tal answered. What do you want?

   _____

3. I want to see the new 3-D movie. said Wendy.

   _____

4. me too replied Jenny. It looks really scary!

   _____

5. It looks as if it might snow said Mrs. Wu.

   _____

6. I hope not replied Mr. Wu. I left my boots at home.

   _____

Punctuate Dialogue

> Dialogue is a conversation between two or more characters. Quotation marks show the exact words a speaker says.
> Use a comma to separate the speaker's introduction or tag from the words he or she says. Place periods inside quotation marks. If the dialogue itself ends in a question mark or an exclamation point, place the punctuation inside the final quotation mark and drop the comma.
>
> "How many children are in your family**?**" **asked Mr. Sanez**.
> **Angela explained,** "I am the youngest of three sisters**.**"
> "I have one brother**,**" Marco said**,** "and one sister."

Rewrite each sentence with correct punctuation.

1. Erik complained There are too many leaves to rake.

2. Would you like some help? asked Raul.

3. Helene groaned I feel really sick.

4. Why did you like that book? Pedro asked.

5. I was born in Russia Yuri explained. Where are you from?

6. I have to run an errand Mara said.

Name _____ Date _____

Punctuate Dialogue

> Dialogue is a conversation between two or more characters. Quotation marks show the exact words a speaker says. Use a comma to separate the speaker's introduction or tag from the words he or she says. Place periods inside quotation marks. If the dialogue itself ends in a question mark or an exclamation point, place the punctuation inside the final quotation mark and drop the comma.
>
> **Bella yawned and said,** "I'm too tired to read another page."
>
> "I'm going to bed, too," agreed Roza. "What time is it?"

Rewrite each sentence with correct punctuation.

1. What time is the concert? Sam asked.

   _____

2. It starts at 7 o'clock answered Liz. But let's get there early.

   _____

3. Mom asked How many friends will be sleeping over?

   _____

4. Only Amar and Beto said Tony. Is that okay?

   _____

5. What time will you be home today? asked Uncle Arturo.

   _____

6. Gino replied I should be home right after band practice.

   _____

Name _____ Date _____

Capitalize Proper Nouns

Common nouns name a general person, place, or thing. Proper nouns name specific people, places, or things. Each main word in a proper noun should begin with a capital letter.

Common Noun	Proper Noun
painting	Mona Lisa
park	Grand Teton National Park
sea	Caribbean Sea

Use the chart below to sort and match each common and proper noun in the box. Write each proper noun with correct capitalization.

state	harry potter	friday	main character
lake erie	continent	california	lake
fairy tale	day	the three little pigs	africa

Common Nouns	Proper Nouns

Name _____ Date _____

Capitalize Proper Nouns

> A proper noun names a specific person, place, or thing. Each main word of a proper noun should begin with a capital letter. The titles and names of people; the days of the week and the months of the year; and specific holidays and names of geographic places are proper nouns.
> **Groundhog Day** is a holiday in **February**.
> On **Tuesday**, **Ivan** will visit the **Museum of Art**.

Circle the proper noun in each sentence. Then rewrite the sentence with correct capitalization for the proper noun.

1. Last summer, we went to new orleans, louisiana.

   _____

2. The grand canyon is an amazing place to visit.

   _____

3. This year, we will celebrate thanksgiving at my grandparent's house.

   _____

4. We saw many boats sailing on lake huron.

   _____

5. My brother wants to climb mount whitney someday.

   _____

6. On independence day, we had a picnic and watched fireworks.

   _____

7. Have you ever seen the magnificent niagara falls?

   _____

Name _____ Date _____

Capitalize Book Titles

> Capitalize the first and last word and each additional main word of a book title. Unless it is the first or last word of the title, do not capitalize the following words: **a**, **an**, and **the**; most short prepositions, such as **at**, **in**, **by**, **for**, **of**, and **to**; and conjunctions such as **and**, **but**, **or**, and **nor**.

Rewrite each book title with correct capitalization.

1. the sword And The stone
   _____

2. island of the blue dolphins
   _____

3. robin hood And his merry Men
   _____

4. charlie and the chocolate factory
   _____

5. tom swift, boy inventor
   _____

6. james and the giant Peach
   _____

7. the wizard of oz
   _____

Name _____ Date _____

Sentence Types

There are four different types of sentences. The end punctuation reveals the sentence type.

Declarative:	statement, or telling sentence	ends in a period **.**
Interrogative:	sentence that asks a question	ends in a question mark **?**
Exclamatory:	sentence that shows strong feeling	ends in an exclamation mark **!**
Imperative:	sentence that gives a command	ends in a period **.**

Read each sentence. Circle the sentence type. Then write the correct end punctuation on the line.

1. Are you trying out for the team _____
   statement   question   exclamation   command

2. I don't know how to play field hockey _____
   statement   question   exclamation   command

3. I can teach you right this minute _____
   statement   question   exclamation   command

4. Hold this field hockey stick _____
   statement   question   exclamation   command

5. I'll roll the ball to you, and you try to hit it with the stick _____
   statement   question   exclamation   command

6. Shouldn't I warm up first _____
   statement   question   exclamation   command

Name _____ Date _____

Fragments and Complete Sentences

A complete sentence contains a subject and a verb, and expresses a complete thought. A sentence fragment is missing a subject, a verb, or both, so it does not express a complete thought. To correct a fragment, add the missing subject or verb.

    The baker a special cake.
    The baker **made** a special cake.

Read each sentence. Write *CS* if it is a complete sentence. If the group of words is a fragment, write what is missing: *subject* or *verb*.

1. _____ The cows at the farm.

2. _____ That movie was hilarious.

3. _____ Made three snowmen.

4. _____ Might miss the math test due to the flu.

5. _____ Big, gray clouds in the sky.

Rewrite each pair of fragments as a complete sentence.

6. Every member of my family. Attended the reunion picnic.

_____

7. My sister and her friends. To the local mall.

_____

Name _____ Date _____

Fragments and Complete Sentences

> A complete sentence contains a subject and a verb, and expresses a complete thought. A sentence fragment is missing a subject, a verb, or both, so it does not express a complete thought. To correct a fragment, add the missing subject or verb.

For each fragment, circle what is missing: *subject* or *verb*. Choose a phrase from the box and rewrite the fragment as a complete sentence.

fell	bloom	our favorite cousin	the ship's captain	a red truck

1. Daffodils, irises, and tulips.
   subject   verb

   _____

2. Announced the news to the passengers.
   subject   verb

   _____

3. Invited us to spend the weekend.
   subject   verb

   _____

4. The leaves swirling in the air.
   subject   verb

   _____

5. Is parked in the driveway.
   subject   verb

   _____

Name _____ Date _____

Use Coordinating Conjunctions to Form Compound Sentences

Use a comma and a coordinating conjunction such as **and**, **or**, **but**, and **so** to combine two sentences to form a compound sentence. The conjunction shows how the two parts of the compound sentence are related. **And** adds information, **or** shows a choice, **but** shows a contrast, and **so** shows a result. Always place a comma before the conjunction.

Do you want pizza. Would you prefer pasta?
Do you want pizza, **or** would you prefer pasta?

Write the correct coordinating conjunctions to show how the parts of the sentence are related. Choose one of the following: *and, or, but,* **or** *so.*

1. Sophia doesn't eat meat, _____ she does eat fish.

2. Jose was feverish, _____ he had a cough.

3. My brother likes fishing, _____ he doesn't like hiking.

4. I might go to the circus, _____ I could go to the movies.

5. Nino's bike had a flat tire, _____ he couldn't ride it.

6. We needed butter, _____ I went to the corner store.

7. Mr. Garcia plays soccer, _____ he coaches volleyball, too.

8. I can walk to my aunt's house, _____ I can take the bus.

Name _____ Date _____

Use Coordinating Conjunctions to Form Compound Sentences

> Use a comma and a coordinating conjunction such as **and**, **or**, **but**, and **so** to combine two sentences to form a compound sentence. The conjunction shows how the two parts of the compound sentence are related. **And** adds information, **or** shows a choice, **but** shows a contrast, and **so** shows a result. Always place a comma before the conjunction.
>
> I enjoy skating. I like bike riding more.
> I enjoy skating**,** **but** I like bike riding more.

Circle the correct conjunction to join each pair of sentences. Then write the compound sentence on the line. Remember to add a comma where needed.

1. Carlos saw a movie last week. He went to a museum.
    and   but   or

    _____

2. I called my father. He won't worry about me.
    but   and   so

    _____

3. Kate can't come over now. She can come over later.
    or   and   but

    _____

4. Should I get a puppy? Should I get an older dog?
    or   so   and

    _____

5. I set my alarm. I'm sure I won't oversleep.
    but   so   and

    _____

Name _____ Date _____

Use Coordinating Conjunctions to Form Compound Sentences

> Use a comma and a coordinating conjunction such as **and**, **or**, **but**, and **so** to combine two sentences to form a compound sentence. The conjunction shows how the two parts of the compound sentence are related. **And** adds information, **or** shows a choice, **but** shows a contrast, and **so** shows a result. Always place a comma before the conjunction.
>
> I like spinach. I don't like kale.
>
> I like spinach, **but** I don't like kale.

Rewrite each pair of sentences to form a compound sentence. Use one of the following coordinating conjunctions: *and, or, but, so.*

1. It was raining hard. The football game was called off.

   _____

2. Omar needs new boots. He just bought a pair of gloves.

   _____

3. I speak Chinese at home. I speak English at school.

   _____

4. I might buy the book. I might take it out at the library.

   _____

5. Rodrigo was thirsty. He got a glass of water.

   _____

Name _____ Date _____

Use Subordinating Conjunctions to Form Complex Sentences

> Use a comma and a subordinating conjunction such as **although**, **because**, **since**, **while**, **if**, **when**, **before**, and **until** to combine two sentences to form a complex sentence.
> I love to visit my aunt **because** she is so much fun.
> I will visit her today **unless** practice runs late.

Circle the correct subordinating conjunction to complete each sentence. Write it on the line.

1. I will save you a seat _____ you get there first.

   although   unless   when

2. Harry said he was sorry _____ I'm not sure he means it.

   after   although   while

3. Please come to the office _____ you arrive.

   when   because   although

4. I don't have enough binders _____ I used them all.

   while   although   because

5. Please try to be quiet _____ the baby wakes up.

   until   because   while

6. I will wash the dishes _____ you cooked dinner.

   before   unless   since

Name _____ Date _____

Use Subordinating Conjunctions to Form Complex Sentences

> Use a comma and a subordinating conjunction such as **although**, **because**, **since**, **while**, **if**, **when**, **before**, and **until** to combine two sentences to form a complex sentence.
> I loved the movie. It was really exciting.
> I loved the movie **because** it was really exciting.

Write the correct subordinating conjunction to complete each sentence. Choose one of the following: *although, because, if, when, before, until.*

1. Please stop at the store _____ it's out of your way.

2. Sunita brushes her teeth _____ she goes to sleep.

3. My dog sits at my feet _____ I eat dinner.

4. Ken practices the piano _____ he doesn't make any mistakes.

5. We can have a pool party _____ it doesn't rain.

6. I did well on the test _____ I studied hard.

7. I go to the movies _____ the weather is bad.

Conquer Grammar • Grade 3 • © Newmark Learning, LLC

Name _____ Date _____

Use Subordinating Conjunctions to Form Complex Sentences

> Use a comma and a subordinating conjunction such as **although**, **because**, **since**, **while**, **if**, **when**, **before**, and **until** to combine two sentences to form a complex sentence.
> We'll play softball **unless** the field is too wet.
> Our dog drinks water **after** he runs in the park.

Rewrite each pair of sentences to form a complex sentence. Use one of the following subordinating conjunctions: *since, unless, while, before, after*.

1. Amy can go to bed late. She is in third grade now.

   _____

2. I changed my sheets. I made my bed.

   _____

3. We can go boating. It stopped raining.

   _____

4. You can't play video games. Finish your chores first.

   _____

5. We will go home. The actors take their bows.

   _____

6. Stefan watched TV. His brother was having his eyes examined.

   _____

   _____

Name _____ Date _____

Compound and Complex Sentences

> Use a comma and a coordinating conjunction such as **and, or, but,** or **so** to join two sentences to make a compound sentence. Use a subordinating conjunction such as **although, because, since,** or **unless** to join two sentences to make a complex sentence.
> **Compound:** Gabe loves to act**, and** he will be in our play.
> **Complex:** Gabe will be in our play **because** he loves to act.

Rewrite each pair of sentences to form a compound sentence. Use the conjunction in the parentheses ( ) and a comma.

1. My brother is good at math. I am good at English.   (and)

   _____

2. It's a very long walk to school. I take the bus.   (so)

   _____

3. Lucas plays soccer. He would rather play the trumpet.   (but)

   _____

Rewrite each pair of sentences to form a complex sentence. Use the conjunction in the parentheses ( ) and a comma.

4. Our tennis match ended. Then it started to rain.   (before)

   _____

5. We will also play tomorrow. We won't if the court is wet. (unless)

   _____

Name _____ Date _____

Compound and Complex Sentences

> Use a comma and a coordinating conjunction such as **and, or, but,** or **so** to join two sentences to make a compound sentence. Use a subordinating conjunction such as **although, because, since,** or **unless** to join two sentences to make a complex sentence.
>
> **Compound:** Mina excels at math, **so** she may become a doctor.
>
> **Complex:** Mina may become a doctor **because** she excels at math.

Underline whether each sentence is compound, or complex. Then circle the conjunction in the sentence.

1. My mother is an immigrant from Spain, but my father was born in Virginia.
   compound   complex

2. My friends come from many countries, and I find it fascinating.
   compound   complex

3. I understand Spanish although we speak English at home.
   compound   complex

4. My family is diverse, so we have Spanish and American traditions.
   compound   complex

5. I am happy because we celebrate many different traditions, too!
   compound   complex

Name _____   Date _____

Compound and Complex Sentences

Use a comma and a coordinating conjunction such as **and, or, but,** or **so** to join two sentences to make a compound sentence. Use a subordinating conjunction such as **although, because, since,** or **unless** to join two sentences to make a complex sentence.

Compound: Ian waited for the bus, **but** it was late.
Complex: Ian waited for the bus **although** it was late.

Underline whether each sentence is compound or complex. Then circle the conjunction in the sentence.

1. I love tortillas, so my grandmother often makes them for me.
   compound   complex

2. Many of my friends have pets, but Mom is allergic.
   compound   complex

3. I enjoy walking my next-door neighbor's dog unless it is raining.
   compound   complex

4. My neighbor across the street also has a dog, and I walk that one, too.
   compound   complex

5. I usually feed the dogs in the afternoon before I go to baseball practice.
   compound   complex

6. Baseball practice lasts for two hours, but today we got out later.
   compound   complex

Name _____ Date _____

Compound and Complex Sentences

> Use a comma and a coordinating conjunction such as **and, or, but,** or **so** to join two sentences to make a compound sentence. Use a subordinating conjunction such as **although, because, since,** or **unless** to join two sentences to make a complex sentence.
>
> **Compound Sentence:** Felipe loves most kinds of pizza, **but** he doesn't care for olives.
>
> **Complex Sentence:** Felipe likes most kinds of pizza **although** he doesn't care for olives.

Underline whether each sentence is compound or complex. Then circle the conjunction in the sentence.

1. I might be a doctor someday, or I might be a teacher.

    compound   complex

2. Mina will stay at the library until her mother picks her up.

    compound   complex

3. Eduardo will dry the dishes after his brother washes them.

    compound   complex

4. Nelly will shop for a dress on Sunday unless she is too tired.

    compound   complex

5. I will help Jack with studying, so he will do well on his test.

    compound   complex

6. The show started late because the lights were broken.

    compound   complex

Name _____ Date _____

Compound and Complex Sentences

> Use a comma and a coordinating conjunction such as **and, or, but,** or **so** to join two sentences to make a compound sentence. Use a subordinating conjunction such as **although, because, since,** or **unless** to join two sentences to make a complex sentence.
>
> **Compound:** Jess likes to play basketball, **but** she likes softball more.
>
> **Complex:** Let's meet at the park **unless** it rains.

Write a coordinating conjunction to complete each compound sentence.

1. Maggie ate lunch late, _____ she wasn't hungry for dinner.

2. Violet is an excellent actress, _____ she is a good singer, too.

Write a subordinating conjunction to complete each complex sentence.

3. I will be in the contest _____ I'm not a good singer.

4. I kept eating raisins _____ there were none left.

5. Andrea will join the team _____ practice conflicts with her trumpet lessons.

6. I asked Mom to pick up some snacks _____ we were so hungry!

Conquer Grammar • Grade 3 • © Newmark Learning, LLC   89

Name _____ Date _____

Standard English

> Standard English follows accepted rules of grammar, punctuation, spelling, and vocabulary. Nonstandard, or conversational, English is used in informal communication, such as in text messages, e-mails, and story dialogue.
>
> **Standard English:** Lillian was very excited to visit her grandmother.
>
> **Nonstandard English:** Lillian was gonna see her grandmother.

Rewrite each sentence. Replace any underlined words with the correct standard English word or phrase from the box.

going on	Are you	hurry up	any
going to	have to	I will see you later	

1. "If you don't <u>move it</u>, we're <u>gonna</u> be late!"

   _____

2. "I can't eat <u>no</u> more!" groaned Margo.

   _____

3. "What's <u>up</u> with Dennis?"

   _____

4. "<u>You</u> kidding me?"

   _____

5. "I <u>gotta</u> go. <u>Catch you later</u>!"

   _____

90   Conquer Grammar • Grade 3 • © Newmark Learning, LLC

Name _____ Date _____

Standard English

> Standard English follows accepted rules of grammar, punctuation, spelling, and vocabulary. Nonstandard, or conversational, English is used in informal communication, such as in text messages, e-mails, and story dialogue.

Read the letter that Beto wrote to his Aunt Alison. Then rewrite the letter to better represent the conventions of standard English.

Hey, Aunt Ali!!! Week 2 at camp is AWESOME!! All the kids are super cool, and I feel like we're already best friends. This week we got to go camping in the woods, I thought it would be scary but we all sang so many songs and ran around and it was the best. Next week we're gonna ride horses! I'll let you know how that goes, I bet it'll be awesome too. —Beto

Answer Key

Page 8

Singular and Plural Nouns

A singular noun names a person, place, or thing. A plural noun names more than one person, place, or thing. Add **s** to the end of most nouns to make them plural.

Singular Noun	Plural Noun
student	students
lesson	lessons
notebook	notebooks

Circle the noun that correctly completes each sentence. Write it on the line.

1. Our teacher asked us to take out a sheet of _paper_.
   ((paper), papers)

2. There are two _teachers_ in this school who are named Mr. Smith!
   (teacher, (teachers))

3. She used brown and green _markers_ to add trees to her picture.
   (marker, (markers))

4. My favorite _book_ is written by Beverly Cleary.
   ((book), books)

5. Mrs. Taylor has extra _pencils_ in a basket if we need to borrow one of them.
   (pencil, (pencils))

Page 9

Irregular Plural Nouns

A plural noun names more than one person, place, or thing. Regular plural nouns end in **s**. Irregular plural nouns do not have any spelling rules or patterns. Some examples of nouns and their irregular plural forms include **goose/geese**, **foot/feet**, and **ox/oxen**.

Complete each sentence with the plural form of the noun in the parentheses ( ).

1. How many _people_ are going to the party? (person)
2. Annie has two pet _mice_ named Lola and Daisy. (mouse)
3. The _women_ were splashing in the swimming pool. (woman)
4. Those _children_ are talking about the same book. (child)
5. Are you waiting for any baby _teeth_ to fall out? (tooth)
6. My dad and the other _men_ cheered the loudest. (man)
7. The flock of _geese_ flew over the park. (geese)
8. We saw _wolves_ at the animal sanctuary. (wolf)

Page 10

Abstract Nouns

Concrete nouns name things that you can see, hear, smell, taste, or touch. **Pizza**, **cloud**, and **friend** are examples of concrete nouns. Abstract nouns name things that cannot be perceived with one of your five senses. **Hunger**, **loyalty**, and **democracy** are examples of abstract nouns.

Choose the correct abstract noun from the box to complete each sentence. Write it on the line.

patriotism	weather	wisdom	generosity
independence	vacation	pleasure	disagreements

1. Mr. Han paid me more than he needed to. His _generosity_ is overwhelming!
2. My family is going to the lake for _vacation_.
3. I hope that the _weather_ on Tuesday will be cool and dry.
4. We march in a parade to show our _patriotism_.
5. On the Fourth of July Americans celebrate the country's _independence_.
6. My little sister and I have our _disagreements_ but we still love each other.
7. I like helping others and get _pleasure_ from doing it.
8. My aunt often gives me advice, she has a deep _wisdom_ about things.

Page 11

Concrete and Abstract Nouns

Concrete nouns name things you can see, hear, smell, touch, or taste. **Piano**, **icicle**, **volunteer**, and **burrito** are examples of concrete nouns. Abstract nouns name things that cannot be perceived with one of your five senses. **Respect**, **friendship**, **childhood**, and **justice** are examples of abstract nouns.

Circle whether the underlined noun in each sentence is concrete or abstract.

1. The history of my grandparents began in Poland.
   concrete (abstract)
2. Mrs. Garcia takes an interest in all her students.
   (concrete) abstract
3. I have a lot of respect for our new principal.
   concrete (abstract)
4. The office of president can change every four to eight years.
   concrete (abstract)
5. I can't wait to visit my mom's office.
   (concrete) abstract

Identify the abstract noun in each sentence. Write it on the line.

6. Aria takes pride in her cooking. _pride_
7. Honesty is important to me. _honesty_
8. We have the freedom to vote on a class song. _freedom_

Answer Key

Page 12

Concrete and Abstract Nouns

Concrete nouns are things you can see, hear, smell, touch, or taste. **Classroom**, **teacher**, **pizza**, **music**, and **sidewalk** are examples of concrete nouns. Abstract nouns are things that cannot be perceived with one of your five senses. **Courage**, **fear**, **curiosity**, **hope**, and **kindness** are examples of abstract nouns.

Determine whether each noun in the box is concrete or abstract. Then write the noun in the correct column of the chart.

| kindness | music | rhythm | scent | shade |
| bravery | happiness | backache | writer | peace |

Concrete Nouns	Abstract Nouns
music	kindness
scent	bravery
shade	rhythm
backache	happiness
writer	peace

Page 13

Concrete and Abstract Nouns

Concrete nouns name things you can see, hear, smell, touch, or taste. **Auditorium**, **sunset**, **cupcake**, and **music** are examples of concrete nouns. Abstract nouns name things that cannot be perceived with one of your five senses. **Truth**, **honesty**, **luck**, **brilliance**, and **delight** are examples of abstract nouns.

Determine whether each noun in the box is concrete or abstract. Then write the noun in the correct column of the chart.

| faith | mountains | disappointment | candidates |
| confidence | kindness | sunlight | sister |

Concrete Nouns	Abstract Nouns
mountains	faith
candidates	disappointment
sunlight	confidence
sister	kindness

Choose the correct noun from the chart above to complete each sentence. Write it on the line.

1. It was a **disappointment** for Juan to miss the game.
2. Thank you for your **kindness** toward our new teammates.
3. My **sister** is five years older than I am.

Page 14

Possessive Nouns

A possessive noun tells who or what owns something.
Use **'s** to show possession for one person, place, or thing.
  Ollie's bike
Use **s'** to show possession for more than one person, place, or thing.
  our **cousins'** house
Use **'s** to show possession for nouns with irregular plural forms.
  the **women's** basketball team

Write the possessive form of each underlined noun.

1. The question of the <u>student</u>   the **student's** question
2. the job of <u>Mr. Wright</u>   **Mr. Wright's** job
3. the barking of their <u>dogs</u>   their **dogs'** barking
4. the dog of your <u>friend</u>   Your **friend's** dog
5. the garden of our <u>neighbors</u>   our **neighbors'** garden
6. the games of the <u>children</u>   the **children's** games
7. the cameras of those <u>tourists</u>   those **tourists'** cameras
8. the meeting of the <u>teachers</u>   the **teachers'** meeting

Page 15

Possessive Nouns

A possessive noun tells who or what owns something.
Use **'s** to show possession for one person, place, or thing.
  Prince's castle
Use **s'** to show possession for more than one person, place, or thing.
  Princes' castles
Use **'s** to show possession for nouns with irregular plural forms.
  Women's locker room

Write the possessive of each underlined noun.

1. the courage of the <u>child</u>   the **child's** courage
2. the math class of <u>Ms. Manel</u>   **Ms. Manel's** math class
3. the cars of your <u>uncle</u>   your **uncle's** cars
4. the brother of my <u>mother</u>   my **mother's** brother

Rewrite each sentence. Replace the underlined words with a possessive.

5. <u>The three kittens of my cat</u> are playful.
   My cat's three kittens are playful.
6. We replaced <u>the batteries of our car</u>.
   We replaced our car's batteries.

Answer Key

Page 16

Possessive Nouns

A possessive noun tells who or what owns something.
Use **'s** to show possession for one person, place, or thing.
  Max's shoes
Use **s'** to show possession for more than one person, place, or thing.
  Flowers' petals
Use **'s** to show possession for nouns with irregular plural forms.
  Men's team

Write the possessive of each underlined noun.

1. the instruments of the band — the <u>band's</u> instruments
2. the toys of our neighbors — our <u>neighbors'</u> toys
3. the hobbies of some people — some <u>people's</u> hobbies
4. the cousin of my father — my <u>father's</u> cousin

Rewrite each sentence. Replace the underlined words with a possessive.

4. The hockey team of the men plays on Monday.
   <u>The men's hockey team plays on Monday.</u>
5. I wash the manes of the horses.
   <u>I wash the horses' manes.</u>

Page 17

Possessive Nouns

A possessive noun tells who or what owns something.
Use **'s** to show possession for one person, place, or thing.
  Billy's shoes
  class's teacher
Use **s'** to show possession for more than one person, place, or thing.
  cars' lights
Use **'s** to show possession for nouns with irregular plural forms.
  Children's home

Rewrite each sentence. Replace the underlined words with a possessive.

1. The seats on the train are really comfortable.
   <u>The train's seats are really comfortable.</u>
2. You can borrow the skateboard that belongs to my brother.
   <u>You can borrow my brother's skateboard.</u>
3. I walk the dogs of my neighbors.
   <u>I walk my neighbors' dogs.</u>
4. This is the table for the children.
   <u>This is the children's table.</u>
5. The rules of the teachers are tough but fair.
   <u>The teachers' rules are tough but fair.</u>

Page 18

Possessive Nouns

A possessive noun tells who or what owns something.
Use **'s** to show possession for one person, place, or thing.
  Ted's coat
Use **s'** to show possession for more than one person, place, or thing.
  Dancers' shoes
Use **'s** to show possession for nouns with irregular plural forms.
  Women's team

Rewrite each sentence. Replace the underlined words with a possessive.

1. The seats in the stadium are blue and red.
   <u>The stadium's seats are blue and red.</u>
2. Long ago, coats that belonged to men were fancy.
   <u>Long ago, men's coats were fancy.</u>
3. The mascots of the teams are different.
   <u>The teams' mascots are different.</u>
4. The arms of the chair are torn.
   <u>The chair's arms are torn.</u>
5. I found a hat belonging to Sid!
   <u>I found Sid's hat!</u>
6. This is the car belonging to my cousins.
   <u>This is my cousins' car.</u>

Page 19

Possessive Nouns

A possessive noun tells who or what owns something.
Use **'s** to show possession for one person, place, or thing.
  Ginny's sunflowers
Use **s'** to show possession for more than one person, place, or thing.
  our **friends'** parents
Use **'s** to show possession for nouns with irregular plural forms.
  the **children's** playground

Rewrite each sentence. Replace the underlined words with a possessive.

1. A father picks up the toys of his toddler.
   <u>A father picks up his toddler's toys.</u>
2. The softball team of the girls practices after school.
   <u>The girls' softball team practices after school.</u>
3. Clothes for men are on sale in that store.
   <u>Men's clothes are on sale in that store.</u>
4. The kittens hid under the bed in the room of Kaylee.
   <u>The kittens hid under the bed in Kaylee's room.</u>
5. The kitchen of my grandmother smelled of freshly baked cookies.
   <u>My grandmother's kitchen smelled of freshly baked cookies.</u>

Answer Key

Page 20

Past Tense Verbs

Past tense verbs tell about actions that already happened. Most past tense verbs end in **ed**.

For most regular verbs, add **-ed** spill + ed spilled
If a verb ends in **e**, add **-d** advance + d advanced
If a verb ends in a vowel and a single consonant, double the consonant and add **-ed** stop + p + ed stopped
If a verb ends in a consonant and **y**, change the **y** to **i** and add **-ed** marry marri + ed married

Write the past tense form of the verb in the parentheses ( ).

1. Yesterday, Renee and I (watch) __watched__ the new show.
2. The baby (cry) __cried__ because he was hungry.
3. Were you (invite) __invited__ to the party?
4. I (spot) __spotted__ my cousins in the crowd.
5. Benjamin Franklin (invent) __invented__ many useful things.
6. It was such a warm day that we (decide) __decided__ to go for a walk.
7. I am not (allow) __allowed__ to go to the store alone.

Page 21

Past Tense Verbs

Rewrite each sentence with the past tense form of the verb in the parentheses ( ).

1. My brother (apply) to five colleges.
   My brother applied to five colleges.
2. Our dad (help) him with his applications.
   Our dad helped him with his applications.
3. He (shout) with joy when he was accepted!
   He shouted with joy when he was accepted!
4. He (worry) that he wouldn't get in.
   He worried that he wouldn't get in.
5. I (hug) him because I was so happy!
   I hugged him because I was so happy!

Page 22

Verb Tenses

A verb is a word that shows action. Present tense verbs tell about something that is happening right now. Past tense verbs tell about something that has already happened. Future tense verbs tell about something that will happen at a later time.
Present: I **help** my family with household chores.
Past: Yesterday, I **helped** my sister sweep the garage.
Future: I **will help** my brother wash dishes.

Choose the correct verb from the box to complete each sentence. Write it on the line.

board	boarded	will board
release	released	will release
welcome	welcomed	will welcome

1. We __boarded__ the ship over an hour ago.
2. The band __will release__ a new album next year.
3. Please __welcome__ Jorge to our book club.
4. My cousins __will welcome__ a new baby in a few months.
5. I __released__ the balloons into the air at the end of my birthday.
6. The passengers __will board__ the plane at 8:00 p.m.

Page 23

Verb Tenses

A verb is a word that shows action. Present tense verbs tell about something that is happening right now. Past tense verbs tell about something that has already happened. Future tense verbs tell about something that will happen at a later time.

Circle the form of the verb that correctly completes each sentence. Write it on the line.

1. The baby __crawled__ around the house.
   crawl (crawled) will crawl
2. Unless it rains, we __will play__ tennis later.
   play played (will play)
3. The audience must __arrive__ at the concert hall on time.
   (arrive) arrived will arrive

Rewrite each sentence with the past tense form of the verb in the parentheses ( ).

4. I (stop) at my friend's house after school.
   I stopped at my friend's house after school.
5. I (try) to make the cake, but it did not taste as good.
   I tried to make the cake, but it did not taste as good.
6. I (fix) the vase by gluing it together.
   I fixed the vase by gluing it together.

Answer Key

Page 24

Irregular Past Tense Verbs

Past tense verbs tell about actions that already happened. Past tense verbs that do not end in **-ed** are irregular.

Circle the verb in the parentheses ( ) that correctly completes each sentence.

1. My parents (buyed **bought**) me a scooter for my birthday.
2. They (**found** finded) the exact kind that I wanted.
3. The scooter (**is** are) not new, but I love it.
4. I (growed **grew**) out of my old scooter last summer.
5. Who (**got** getted) your scooter for you?
6. We (is **are**) both so lucky to have scooters!
7. Our friends (**made** maked) us cases for our scooters.
8. I (have **had**) fun riding my scooter yesterday.
9. Jenna (rided **rode**) her scooter, too.
10. We (**went** go) to the park for lunch.
11. We (sit **sat**) on a bench and (drink **drank**) water.
12. Elizabeth decided to (**leave** left) early.

Page 25

Irregular Past Tense Verbs

Past tense verbs tell about actions that already happened. Past tense verbs that do not end in **-ed** are irregular. Some examples of verbs and their irregular past tense forms include **to be/was**, **have/had**, **find/found**, **grow/grew**, **buy/bought**, **get/got**, and **make/made**.

Circle the verb in the parentheses ( ) that correctly completes each sentence. Write it on the line.

1. My friends and I __made__ banana bread yesterday. (maked, **made**)
2. It __was__ really tasty. (**was**, be)
3. Kira's mom __got__ the ingredients for us. (get, **got**)
4. She __bought__ almost everything at the grocery store near the mall. (**bought**, buyed)
5. She __had__ to go to another store for the spices. (**had**, haved)
6. Luckily, she __found__ them! (finded, **found**)
7. My brothers __were__ happy when I gave them a taste! (**were**, is)
8. We __grew__ tomatoes over the summer. (**grew**, growed)

Page 26

Irregular Past Tense Verbs

Past tense verbs tell about actions that already happened. Past tense verbs that do not end in **-ed** are irregular. Some examples of verbs and their irregular past tense forms include **keep/kept**, **find/found**, **buy/bought**, and **make/made**.

Write the past tense form of the verb in the parentheses ( ).

1. I __grew__ two inches in the last year. (grow)
2. I __found__ that most of my clothes were too small. (find)
3. My dad __bought__ me some new clothes at the mall. (buy)
4. The bright colors __made__ me happy! (make)
5. I __wore__ my new sandals yesterday. (wear)
6. It __was__ so hot outside! (to be)
7. My sandals __kept__ my feet cool. (keep)

Page 27

Irregular Past Tense Verbs

Past tense verbs tell about actions that already happened. Past tense verbs that do not end in **-d** or **-ed** are irregular. Some examples of verbs and their irregular past tense forms include **find/found**, **grow/grew**, **buy/bought**, **get/got**, and **make/made**.

Write the correct form of the verb in the parentheses ( ) to complete each sentence.

1. We __got__ a foot of snow on the first day of spring last year. (get)
2. My dad woke me up late because I __had__ no school. (have)
3. Austin and I __made__ a snow fort in the front yard. (make)
4. We __found__ tree branches to use as flags for the fort. (find)
5. The tree branches __were__ already on the ground. (to be)
6. That spring, the flowers __grew__ right through the snow! (grow)
7. It was lucky that we __bought__ a new shovel. (buy)
8. Today is the first day of spring, and it __was__ warm and sunny. (to be)

Answer Key

Page 28

Irregular Past Tense Verbs

Past tense verbs tell about actions that already happened. Past tense verbs that do not end in -ed are irregular. Some examples of verbs and their irregular past tense forms include:

Present Tense	Irregular Past Tense
grow	grew
make	made
find	found
get	got
buy	bought

Choose the correct verb from the box to complete each sentence. Write it on the line.

grow	make	grew	made	found
find	get	buy	got	bought

1. Tina __grew__ four inches in the last year.
2. Stephen and Alex __made__ dinner for their grandma.
3. I __bought__ my cousin a gift with the money I saved.
4. I misplaced your ball and have not __found__ it yet.
5. I __got__ a chill after I went out without a coat.
6. Who __grew__ these lovely flowers?
7. I need to __find__ my notebook.

Page 29

Irregular Past Tense Verbs

Past tense verbs tell about actions that already happened. Past tense verbs that do not end in -ed are irregular.

Choose the correct verb from the box to complete each sentence. Write it on the line.

am	was	were	make
made	grew	found	had

1. I __had__ a kickball game last Sunday.
2. My dad __made__ the team's uniforms.
3. Tito __was__ the catcher last year.
4. This year, I __am__ pitching.
5. The ball got lost, but then the coach __found__ it.

Rewrite each sentence with the past tense form of the underlined verb.

6. When she had a garden, my aunt grows different vegetables.
   When she had a garden, my aunt grew different vegetables.
7. The ice cream store makes many types of flavors.
   The ice cream store made many types of flavors.

Page 30

Irregular and Regular Past Tense Verbs

Past tense verbs tell about actions that already happened. Past tense verbs that do not end in -d or -ed are irregular. Some examples of verbs and their irregular past tense forms include have/had, grow/grew, find/found, and make/made.

Rewrite each sentence. Replace the underlined verb with the past tense form. There is a mix of regular and irregular verbs.

1. We will have our first soccer game on Saturday.
   We had our first soccer game on Saturday.
2. We are in first place in the league.
   We were in first place in the league.
3. I am the goalie and team captain.
   I was the goalie and team captain.
4. Maria makes all her penalty shots.
   Maria made all her penalty shots.
5. Maria hopes to be the team captain.
   Maria hoped to be the team captain.
6. She will grow three inches taller this year!
   She grew three inches taller this year!
7. Maria and I find that being tall helps to block goals.
   Maria and I found that being tall helps to block goals.

Page 31

Irregular Verbs: to be and have

Past tense verbs that do not end in -ed are irregular. **To be** and **have** are examples of verbs with irregular past tense and plural forms.

to be			have		
Singular	Present	Past	Singular	Present	Past
I	am	was	I	have	had
you	are	were	you	have	had
he/she/it	is	was	he/she/it	has	had
Plural			Plural		
we	are	were	we	have	had
they	are	were	they	have	had

Circle the correct verb in the parentheses ( ). Write the complete sentence on the line.

1. David ((is) are) coming over today.
   David is coming over today.
2. I ((am) was) getting some snacks ready now.
   I am getting some snacks ready now.
3. Jamal and Kendra (was (were)) here yesterday.
   Jamal and Kendra were here yesterday.
4. They (have (had)) a lot of fun!
   They had a lot of fun!

Answer Key

Page 32

Subject-Verb Agreement

The subject of a sentence is a noun that tells whom or what the sentence is about. The verb tells what the subject does. The subject and the verb in a sentence must agree. A singular subject takes a singular verb. A plural subject takes a plural verb. Most singular verbs end in **s**. Removing the final **s** from the verbs makes the verbs plural.
  Singular Subject: Those <u>boys</u> **play** baseball.
  Plural Subject: That <u>girl</u> **plays** tennis.

Determine whether the subject of each sentence is singular or plural. Circle the correct verb. Then write it on the line.

1. Anthony ____places____ the bowls on the top shelf.
   (place, (places))

2. Mia ____plays____ the flute, and she is very talented.
   (play, (plays))

3. My cousins ____sing____ in the chorus.
   ((sing), sings)

4. Trevon ____reads____ many science books.
   (read, (reads))

5. The flowers ____smell____ so sweet!
   ((smell), smells)

Page 33

Subject-Verb Agreement

The subject of a sentence is a noun that tells whom or what the sentence is about. The verb tells what the subject does. The subject and the verb in a sentence must agree. A singular subject takes a singular verb. A plural subject takes a plural verb. Most singular verbs end in **s**. Removing the final **s** from the verbs makes the verbs plural.
  Singular Subject: <u>Katie</u> **loves** her brothers very much.
  Plural Subject: <u>Fred and Tito</u> **love** their sister, too.

Determine whether the subject of each sentence is singular or plural. Circle the correct verb. Then write the complete sentence on the line.

1. Marisol (practice, (practices)) the piano every day.
   Mara practices the piano every day.

2. All the students (takes, (take)) the subway to the museum.
   All the students take the subway to the museum.

3. We ((recycle), recycles) paper and plastic at school.
   We recycle paper and plastic at school.

4. Both of my cats ((hide), hides) under my bed.
   Both of my cats hide under my bed.

5. He (hear, (hears)) you talking from across the room.
   He hears you talking from across the room.

Page 34

Subject-Verb Agreement

The subject of a sentence is a noun that tells whom or what the sentence is about. The verb tells what the subject does. The subject and the verb in a sentence must agree. A singular subject takes a singular verb. A plural subject takes a plural verb. Most singular verbs end in **s**. Removing the final **s** from the verbs makes the verbs plural.
  Singular Subject: <u>Charlie</u> **enjoys** going to the beach.
  Plural Subject: <u>Alexi and Moira</u> **enjoy** the ocean.

Determine whether the subject of each sentence is singular or plural. Circle the correct verb. Then write the complete sentence on the line.

1. Mr. Torres (coach, (coaches)) our baseball team.
   Mr. Torres coaches our baseball team.

2. Jordan (use, (uses)) a list to shop for groceries.
   Jordan uses a list to shop for groceries.

3. Our parents ((drive), drives) very carefully.
   Our parents drive very carefully.

4. The twins both ((play), plays) musical instruments.
   The twins both play musical instruments.

5. When I can't reach the top shelf, I ((ask), asks) for help.
   When I can't reach the top shelf, I ask for help.

Page 35

Subject-Verb Agreement

The subject of a sentence is a noun that tells whom or what the sentence is about. The verb tells what the subject does. The subject and the verb in a sentence must agree. A singular subject takes a singular verb. A plural subject takes a plural verb. Most singular verbs end in **s**. Removing the final **s** from the verbs makes the verbs plural.
  Singular Subject: <u>The meal</u> **is** spicy.
  Plural Subject: <u>My brothers</u> **are** very kind.

Rewrite each sentence with the correct subject-verb agreement.

1. Ella water the flowers in her garden.
   Ella waters the flowers in her garden.

2. Gino and Mary works in the same office.
   Gino and Mary work in the same office.

3. My cousin walk his new dog.
   My cousin walks his new dog.

4. My mom and dad wants to take the family on vacation.
   My mom and dad want to take the family on vacation.

5. When it's sunny outside, I rides my bicycle.
   When it's sunny outside, I ride my bicycle.

Answer Key

Page 36

Subject and Object Pronouns

A pronoun takes the place of a subject or object in a sentence. **I, you, he, she, it, we,** and **they** are subject pronouns. Use a subject pronoun when a pronoun is the subject of a sentence (**me** and **you** can be both object and subject pronouns). **Me, you, him, her, it, us,** and **them** are object pronouns. You and it can be both. Use an object pronoun when a pronoun is the object of a verb or a preposition.

Subject Pronoun: Ricky went outside. **He** took a walk.
Object Pronoun: Ariel saw Mr. Miller. She waved to **him**.

Underline the subject of the first sentence. Circle the pronoun in the second sentence that replaces it.

1. The <u>principal</u> walked down the hallway. (She) greeted every student by name.
2. <u>Michael and Jason</u> studied together. (They) both got a good score on this test.
3. Saturday, <u>Jenna</u> went to a party. (She) had a wonderful time.
4. This summer, the local <u>pool</u> will reopen. (It) will be a good place to keep cool.

Circle the object of the first sentence. Underline the pronoun in the second sentence that replaces it.

5. Mom invited our (cousins) to spend the weekend. My brother took <u>them</u> swimming.
6. Jack and Abby happily joined (my brother). Both cousins like <u>him</u> a lot.
7. The lifeguard blew a (whistle). The swimmers heard <u>it</u> and left the pool.

Page 37

Pronoun-Antecedent Agreement

The noun that a pronoun replaces is called an antecedent. A pronoun and its antecedent must match in number and person. In the example below, **Maria, her,** and **she** match because they all refer to one girl.

Maria lost **her** scarf, but **she** found it at the end of the day.

Circle the correct pronoun and write it on the line. Then underline the antecedent.

1. <u>Lorenzo</u> went to see ___his___ math tutor after school.
   her (his) their
2. The <u>boys</u> will play ___their___ first game on Sunday.
   its his (their)
3. Will you please wash the <u>dishes</u> and put ___them___ away?
   our (them) her
4. I will do my <u>homework</u> now and hand ___it___ in tomorrow.
   (it) he them
5. <u>Marco</u> is leaving soon. I will really miss ___him___.
   (him) her them
6. <u>Sue</u>, please put ___your___ shoes away so I don't trip on them!
   me you (your)

Page 38

Pronoun-Antecedent Agreement

The noun that a pronoun replaces is called an antecedent. A pronoun and its antecedent must match in number and person. In the example below, **Sergio, his,** and **he** match because they all refer to one boy.

Sergio went to **his** class, and **he** sat in **his** seat.

Choose the correct pronoun from the box to complete each sentence. Write it on the line. Make sure the pronoun and its antecedent agree.

you	your	he	him	she
her	they	their	we	our

1. Troy, will ___you___ please stop bothering me?
2. Arjun and Ahmed are going to help ___their___ dad rake.
3. I will take care of my brother when ___he___ wakes up.
4. Andy and I are best friends, so ___we___ do everything together.
5. I tried to call Marco, but I can't reach ___him___.
6. Natalie, is this ___your___ backpack?

Page 39

Possessive Pronouns

A possessive pronoun shows who or what owns something. **My, mine, your, yours, her, hers, his, its, our, ours, their,** and **theirs** are possessive pronouns. A possessive pronoun never has an apostrophe.

This is not **my** binder. That red one is **mine**.
This sweater is **hers**. I will take it to **her** house tomorrow.

Circle the possessive pronoun that correctly completes each sentence.

1. Kayla opened (its, (her)) bedroom window.
2. The excited dog wagged ((its), their) tail.
3. The students rode ((their), theirs) skateboards after school.
4. Lilly, is this pencil (your, (yours))?
5. I finished every book on ((my), mine) summer reading list.
6. ((Our), Ours) aunt always makes me laugh.
7. ((Their), Mine) cat is the friendliest cat I know.
8. Sam, I found (yours, (your)) coat!

Answer Key

Page 40

Indefinite Pronouns

Indefinite pronouns take the place of a noun or noun phrase in a sentence. Indefinite pronouns do not refer to specific people, places, or things. Some examples of indefinite pronouns include **everyone, everything, anyone, anywhere, anything, someone, somewhere, something, no one, nowhere, nothing**.

Choose the correct pronoun in the parentheses ( ) to complete each sentence. Write the sentence on the line.

1. My kind mother will help (anyone, no one) who is deserving.
   My kind mother will help anyone who is deserving.
2. There is (anyone, no one) kinder than my mother.
   There is no one kinder than my mother.
3. Because we love the beach, we will go (somewhere, nowhere) near an ocean.
   Because we love the beach, we will go somewhere near an ocean.
4. (Anyone, Everyone) was happy to see the clouds parting.
   Everyone was happy to see the clouds parting.
5. (Nothing, Everything) makes me laugh more than a funny movie.
   Nothing makes me laugh more than a funny movie.

Page 41

Reflexive Pronouns

Reflexive pronouns refer back to the subject of a sentence and always end in **-self** or **-selves**. **Myself, yourself, himself, herself, itself, ourselves, yourselves**, and **themselves** are reflexive pronouns.
   I bought **myself** a toy.

Write a reflexive pronoun to complete each sentence.

1. I bought ___myself___ a comic book.
2. They baked those cookies ___themselves___.
3. Joshua poured ___himself___ a glass of water.
4. Malina built the dresser ___herself___.
5. The friends asked ___themselves___ if they should see the scary movie or the comedy.
6. Jake and I made ___ourselves___ a tasty dinner.
7. The cat cleaned ___itself___ after it came in from the rain.
8. You can solve the math problem ___yourself___.

Page 42

Reciprocal Pronouns

Use the reciprocal pronoun **each other** to refer to two people or things performing the same action toward each other. Use the reciprocal pronoun **one another** to refer to three or more people or things performing the same action toward one another.
   Joe and Mario were happy to see **each other**.
   We and all the visitors greeted **one another**.

Write the reciprocal pronoun that correctly completes the sentence: *each other* or *one another*.

1. My brother and my father look just like ___each other___.
2. All the people in the crowded subway were bumping against ___one another___.
3. When you meet a new teammate, you should tell ___each other___ your names.
4. Can we all agree to get along with ___one another___?
5. The team members shook hands with ___one another___ after the game.
6. I cannot believe it has been one whole year since you and I have seen ___each other___.

Page 43

Reciprocal Pronouns

Reciprocal pronouns help eliminate repetitive sentences or repetition within a sentence. Use the reciprocal pronoun **each other** to show that two people or things are performing the same action toward each other. Use the reciprocal pronoun **one another** to refer to three or more people or things performing the same action toward one another.
   They looked at **each other**.
   The teachers and students respect **one another**.

Rewrite the sentence or sentences using *each other* or *one another*.

1. Brad will meet Yolanda at the movies. Yolanda will meet Brad at the movies.
   Brad and Yolanda will meet each other at the movies.
2. My dog loves my cat, and my cat loves my dog.
   My dog and cat love each other.
3. All the children stared at the owls, and all the owls stared at the children.
   All the children and owls stared at one another.
4. Matt passed the ball to Kit. Kit passed the ball to Matt.
   Matt and Kit passed the ball to each other.
5. The members of the team thanked the fans, and the fans thanked the members of the team.
   The members of the team and the fans thanked one another.

Answer Key

Page 44

Reciprocal Pronouns

Use a reciprocal pronoun when two or more people or things are performing the same action and are both affected by the action in the same way. Use **each other** to refer to two people or things. Use **One another** to refer to three or more people or things.
 Bella and Drew smiled at **each other**.
 After the game, all the players high-fived **one another**.

Rewrite each sentence with the reciprocal pronoun *each other* or *one another*.

1. Abby admired Manny, and Manny admired Abby.
   Abby and Manny admired each other.
2. Each musician complimented all the other musicians.
   All the musicians complimented one another.
3. My dad usually agrees with my mom, and my mom usually agrees with my dad.
   My dad and mom usually agree with each other.
4. My cat gets along with my two dogs. My two dogs get along with my cat.
   My cat and my two dogs get along with one another.
5. Tanya took turns writing to Noel. Noel took turns writing to Tanya.
   Tanya and Noel took turns writing to each other.

Page 45

Adjectives

Adjectives are words that describe nouns. An adjective may express an opinion or describe the look or feel of the noun, its age, color, origin, or the material it is made of.

Opinion: a **tasty** meal Look or feel: a **kind** friend
Age: an **old** piano Color: a **red** apple
Origin: an **Australian** flag Material: a **cotton** shirt
Size: a **big** house Shape: a **round** clock

Circle the adjective in each sentence. Underline the noun it describes.

1. The (tiny) puppy had a lot of energy.
2. Sara sat on the (comfortable) chair.
3. The (brown) branches and the (green) leaves of the tree shaded us from the sun.
4. We found a ladybug on the (wooden) fence.

Complete each sentence. Write an adjective that matches the category in the parentheses ( ).
Sample answers are provided.

5. This *blue* sweater is my favorite. (color)
6. Pages from the *ancient* book fell out. (age)
7. We ate *spicy* food at the party. (opinion)

Page 46

Adjectives

Adjectives are words that describe nouns. An adjective may express an opinion or describe the look or feel of the noun, its age, color, origin, or the material it is made of.

Opinion: a **fancy** house Look or feel: a **shiny** apple
Age: an **eight-year-old** girl Color: a **yellow** lemon
Origin: an **American** flag Material: a **metal** shelf
Size: a **small** cat Shape: a **square** table

Circle the adjective in each sentence. Underline the noun it describes.

1. This (newborn) baby is my sister.
2. The family went to an (Italian) restaurant.
3. (Artistic) students entered their work in the competition.
4. We shopped for groceries at a (local) store.

Complete each sentence. Write an adjective that matches the category in the parentheses ( ).
Sample answers are provided.

5. He sat on the *soft* rug in the living room. (look/feel)
6. I must return this *interesting* book to the library. (opinion)
7. The *brick* house was beautiful. (material)

Page 47

Adverbs

Adverbs give more information about where or when an action occurs or how it happens. An adverb can appear before or after the verb it modifies or in between different verb parts.
 Where: The wind was blowing leaves **everywhere**.
 When: **Later**, we will watch a movie.
 How: The children were laughing **loudly**.

Circle the adverb in each sentence. Then write if it shows *where*, *when*, or *how* the action happens.

1. My little brother splashed (happily) in the wading pool. *how*
2. We sat (comfortably) on the soft cushions. *how*
3. I walk my dog (daily). *when*
4. Our volleyball team practices (indoors). *where*
5. I will celebrate my birthday (soon). *when*
6. The detective (cleverly) solved the case. *how*
7. The music classroom is (upstairs). *where*
8. Yesterday, I bought a new shirt. *when*

Answer Key

Page 48

Adverbs

Adverbs give more information about where or when an action occurs or how it happens. An adverb can appear before or after the verb it modifies or in between different verb parts. Adverbs can also modify an adjective or another adverb. In those cases, the adverb should appear before the word it modifies.
  Modifies a verb: The rain *fell* **gently**.
  Modifies an adjective: This is a **slightly** *spicy* dinner.
  Modifies another adverb: Our turtle moves **very** *slowly*.

Circle the adverb in each sentence. Underline the word it describes.

1. Our teacher *thought* we would do (quite) *well* on the test.
2. She *ran* (quickly) down the soccer field.
3. These are (incredibly) *fluffy* blankets.
4. Chris *climbed* the tree (skillfully).

Complete each sentence. Write an adjective that matches the category in the parentheses ( ).
Sample answers are provided.

5. We like to play __outside__. (where)
6. I __usually__ walk the dog with my brother. (when)
7. This jacket fits __perfectly__. (how)

Page 49

Adjectives and Adverbs

Adjectives describe, or tell more about, nouns.
  Sasha is a **thoughtful** friend. He sent Reba a **dozen yellow** daisies.
Adverbs describe or tell more about verbs, adjectives, and other adverbs.
  The bus *drove* **very slowly** up the street. Then it *stopped* **completely**.

Circle whether the word in dark type is an adjective or an adverb. Then underline the word it describes.

1. Yesterday at school, the track team had an **important** *race*.
   (adjective) adverb
2. Jenna *sprinted* **away** from the starting point.
   adjective (adverb)
3. In the beginning of the race, she held an **enormous** *lead*.
   (adjective) adverb
4. We all **mistakenly** *believed* that she would win.
   adjective (adverb)
5. However, she **quickly** *fell* behind the other runners.
   adjective (adverb)

Page 50

Adjectives and Adverbs

Adjectives describe, or tell more about, nouns. Some examples of adjectives include **green**, **tall**, **scared**, **wealthy**, **sour**, and **intelligent**. Adverbs describe, or tell more about, verbs, adjectives, and other adverbs. Some examples of adverbs include **honestly**, **foolishly**, **kindly**, **usually**, **very**, **down**, and **up**.

Circle the adjective in each sentence. Underline the word it describes.

1. We approached the (scariest) *house* I have ever seen.
2. Melvin walked up the (crumbling) *steps*.
3. He knocked on the (ancient) *door*.
4. "Who's there?" called out a (spooky) *voice*.

Circle the adverb in each sentence. Underline the word it describes.

5. Melvin *gasped* (loudly).
6. He *ran* (quickly) down the steps, with fear on his face.
7. Melvin's adventure *ended* (badly)!

Page 51

Commas

Within a sentence, commas are used to set off introductory words or phrases, separate words in a series or list, and divide two independent clauses joined by a coordinating conjunction such as **and** or **but**.

  Wow, that was such an exciting adventure movie!
  I have to buy lemons, limes, sugar, and a pitcher.
  It started to rain, but Sergio had his umbrella.

Rewrite each sentence. Add commas where needed.

1. Earlier the doorbell rang.
   Earlier, the doorbell rang.
2. Nicole Marcus and Tommy had arrived.
   Nicole, Marcus, and Tommy had arrived.
3. Tommy wanted to do homework but Nicole wanted to watch funny videos.
   Tommy wanted to do homework, but Nicole wanted to watch funny videos.
4. We took out our textbooks our notes and our pencils.
   We took out our textbooks, our notes, and our pencils.
5. The next thing we knew our work was done and we could watch some videos.
   The next thing we knew, our work was done, and we could watch some videos.
6. Marcus recommended his favorites and we spent the rest of the afternoon laughing.
   Marcus recommended his favorites, and we spent the rest of the afternoon laughing.

Answer Key

Page 52

Comparatives

Comparative adjectives and adverbs compare two people, places, or things. Follow these spelling rules to form comparative adjectives or adverbs: Add **-er** to the end of the adjective or adverb: **taller**. If the word ends in **-y**, change the **y** to **i** and then add **-er**: **prettier**. If the word ends in **-e**, just add **-r**: **later**. If the word ends in a single vowel and a consonant, double the consonant and add **-er**: **bigger**. For longer adjectives or adverbs, add the word **more** in front of the adjective or adverb: **more interesting**.

Write the comparative form of the underlined adjective or adverb. You may need to change the spelling of the word.

1. Gabby and Eve are hard workers, but Eve works _harder_.
2. This spring is rainy, but last spring was _rainier_.
3. Justine likes sweet apples. Which one is _sweeter_ —the green or the red?
4. My dog is big, but my neighbor's dog is even _bigger_.
5. This winter is cold, but last winter was _colder_.
6. I knew the movie would be funny, but it was _funnier_ than I expected!
7. The last soccer coach was strict, but this one is even _stricter_.

Page 53

Superlatives

Superlative adjectives or adverbs compare three or more people, places, or things. Follow these spelling rules to form superlative adjectives or adverbs: Add **-est** to the end of the adjective or adverb: **tallest**. If the word ends in **-y**, change the **y** to **i** and then add **-est**: **prettiest**. If the word ends in **-e**, just add **-st**: **latest**. If the word ends in a single vowel and a consonant, double the consonant and add **-est**: **biggest**. For longer adjectives or adverbs, add the word **most** in front of the adjective or adverb: **most interesting**.

Write the superlative form of the underlined adjective or adverb. You may need to change the spelling of the word.

1. I have heard many noisy birds, but this one is the _noisiest_.
2. Mom wants a big pumpkin. She asked me to get the _biggest_ one I could find.
3. I like hot peppers! Which of these is the _hottest_?
4. That tree is tall. It is the _tallest_ tree I have ever seen.
5. You were so brave! That was the _bravest_ thing you have done.
6. Of all the sad movies I have seen, this one is the _saddest_.
7. The puppies are so little. I want the _littlest_ one!

Page 54

Comparatives and Superlatives

Comparative adjectives and adverbs compare two people, places, or things. Superlative adjectives or adverbs compare three or more people, places, or things. Follow these rules to form comparatives and superlatives:
1. Add **-er** or **-est** to the end of the adjective or adverb.
   Comparative Superlative
   small smaller smallest
2. For longer adjectives or adverbs, add the word **more** or **most** in front of the adjective or adverb.
   Comparative Superlative
   artistic more artistic most artistic
3. Some comparatives and superlatives are irregular and do not follow a pattern. For example:
   Comparative Superlative
   good better best

Write the comparative form of the underlined adjective or adverb.

1. This kitten is adorable, but the black one is _more adorable_.
2. This sweater is cozy, but that blanket is even _cozier_!
3. I enjoy a good puzzle. Which of these two is _better_?

Write the superlative form of the underlined adjective or adverb.

4. Bike trails can be dangerous. Which one is the _most dangerous_?
5. I am so happy! This is the _happiest_ I've ever been!
6. This bowl is large, but that bowl is the _largest_ I have ever seen!

Page 55

Comparatives and Superlatives

Follow these rules to form comparative and superlative adjectives and adverbs:
1. Add **-er** or **-est** to the end of the adjective or adverb.
   Comparative Superlative
   wise wiser wisest
2. For longer adjectives or adverbs, add the word **more** or **most** in front of the adjective or adverb.
   Comparative Superlative
   carefully more carefully most carefully
3. Some comparatives and superlatives are irregular and do not follow a pattern. For example:
   Comparative Superlative
   bad worse worst

Circle the comparative or superlative that correctly completes each sentence. Write it on the line.

1. Yesterday, I saw the _worst_ movie I have ever seen! most bad (worst)
2. Which are the _most delicious_ —the apples, the oranges, or the blueberries? (most delicious) more delicious
3. The mayor is the _most important_ official in city government. more important (most important)
4. I am much _better_ at basketball than bowling. (better) best
5. My green shirt is _more colorful_ than my white one. most colorful (more colorful)

Answer Key

Page 56

Comparatives and Superlatives

Write the comparative or superlative of the word in the parentheses ( ). You may need to change the spelling of the word.

1. There are so many choices! Which kind of yogurt do you like __best__? (good)
2. I like both vanilla and blueberry yogurt, but I like vanilla __better__. (good)
3. I think this striped sweater is __more attractive__ than the plaid one. (attractive)
4. That's the __ugliest__ scarf in the store! (ugly)
5. Ms. Juarez is the __most popular__ teacher in my school. (popular)

Page 57

Comparatives and Superlatives

Write the comparative or superlative of the word in the parentheses ( ). You may need to change the spelling of the word.

1. Which of these two pictures did you like __better__? (good)
2. That is the __tiniest__ pony I have ever seen! (tiny)
3. The yellow chair is much __more comfortable__ than the blue one. (comfortable)
4. That's the __best__ I've ever done on a test! (good)
5. My uncle Roberto is the __wisest__ person I know. (wise)
6. I'm __closer__ in age to my older sister than to my younger one. (close)
7. This is the __most disgusting__ food I've ever tasted! (disgusting)

Page 58

Comparatives and Superlatives

Circle the incorrect word in each sentence. Write the correct comparative or superlative on the line.

1. I think your explanation is (confusinger) than mine. __more confusing__
2. These are the (beautifulest) paintings in the art gallery. __most beautiful__
3. Which yogurt do you think is (gooder)—blueberry or coffee? __better__
4. A storm on field day? This is the (baddest) day ever! __worst__
5. Who is your (goodest) friend on the team? __best__
6. I'm (embarrasseder) now than I was before. __more embarrassed__

Page 59

Prepositions

Write a preposition to begin the prepositional phrase that answers the question in the parentheses ( ).
Sample answers are provided.

1. __After__ dinner, Edgar washed the dishes. (When?)
2. The magazine __with__ the shiny cover belongs to me. (Which one?)
3. It has been raining __for__ several hours. (How long?)
4. Peter knocked over the vase __with__ his backpack. (How?)
5. I always put my bike away __in__ the garage. (Where?)
6. The girl __with__ the red dress is my sister. (Which one?)

Answer Key

Page 60

Prepositions

A prepositional phrase is a group of words that usually includes a preposition and a noun or pronoun along with any modifiers. Only object pronouns can be used in prepositional phrases.
- **Incorrect:** Sean practiced soccer kicks with **I**.
- **Correct:** Sean practiced soccer kicks with **me**.
- **Incorrect:** Sean practiced soccer kicks with Crystal and **I**.
- **Correct:** Sean practiced soccer kicks with **Crystal** and **me**. Sean practiced soccer kicks with **her** and **me**.

Underline the preposition in each sentence. Then circle the correct pronoun or pronouns in the parentheses ( ).

1. Laurel threw the ball <u>between</u> Macy and (I, (me)).
2. Then I threw the ball <u>toward</u> (she, (her)).
3. In the first thirty minutes, no one scored a run <u>except</u> Macy, Laurel, and (I, (me)).
4. Did your mom wave <u>to</u> (he, (him)) and (they, (them))?
5. Yes, and my whole family cheered <u>for</u> (we, (us)).
6. Macy likes playing soccer on the same team <u>with</u> Laurel and (I, (me)).
7. After the game, I had ice cream <u>with</u> (she, (her)).

Page 61

Prepositions

A prepositional phrase is a group of words that usually includes a preposition and a noun or pronoun along with any modifiers. Prepositional phrases often answer questions such as **which one? where? when? how? how long?**
- **Which one?** Minna broke the cup **with** the blue handle.
- **Where?** Put your book **on** the shelf.
- **When?** My grandmother will visit **in** the summer.
- **How?** Our teacher spoke **with** great excitement.
- **How long?** I walked **for** an hour.

Underline the preposition in each sentence. Then circle the word in the parentheses ( ) that tells which question the prepositional phrase answers.

1. Regina raked all the leaves <u>in</u> the yard. ((where) how)
2. My sister planted tulips <u>behind</u> our house. (which one (where))
3. I hope I can go swimming <u>during</u> my vacation. (how long (when))
4. Natalie was wearing a jacket <u>with</u> blue stripes. (when (which one))
5. Eduardo went camping <u>for</u> the weekend. (which one (how long))
6. Can you bring me the book <u>on</u> the desk? (how long (where))

Page 62

Conjunctions

Use a comma and a conjunction such as **and, or, but,** and **so** to combine two sentences to form a compound sentence. Place the comma before the conjunction.
- Byron played baseball. Jerry played soccer.
- Byron played baseball, **and** Jerry played soccer.

Combine each pair of sentences to form one compound sentence. Use a comma and the conjunction in the parentheses ( ). Write the sentence on the line.

1. I like yogurt. I eat it often. (so)
   I like yogurt, so I eat it often.
2. Jake and Tommy are friends. They are in the same class. (and)
   Jake and Tommy are friends, and they are in the same class.
3. Angela likes roller coasters. I prefer Ferris wheels. (but)
   Angela likes roller coasters, but I prefer Ferris wheels.
4. Lilly can bike near the beach. She can bike in the park. (or)
   Lilly can bike near the beach, or she can bike in the park.
5. Mr. Dibo coaches the football team. He conducts the choir. (and)
   Mr. Dibo coaches the football team, and he conducts the choir.
6. I can meet you on Saturday. Sunday would be a better day. (but)
   I can meet you on Saturday, but Sunday would be a better day.

Page 63

Commas for Greetings and Closings

Letters or e-mails begin with a greeting and end with a closing. A greeting consists of a word such as **Dear** or **Hi** and the name of the person you are writing to, followed by a comma. Every word in a greeting should begin with a capital letter.
- **Dear** Mrs. Bryant, **Hi** Carmelo, **Hello**, James,

A closing consists of a word or words such as **Yours, Yours truly, Love,** or **Sincerely** followed by a comma, and the author's name on the next line. Only the first word in a closing should begin with a capital letter.
- Yours,   Lots of love,   Sincerely,
  Michelle   Mom   Ms. Marlon

Circle whether each group of words is a greeting or a closing. Then rewrite it correctly on the lines.

1. Hello Emily — ((greeting) closing) — Hello, Emily,
2. Fondly Sam — (greeting (closing)) — Fondly, Sam
3. Dear Grandma — ((greeting) closing) — Dear Grandma,
4. Your pal Dan — (greeting (closing)) — Your pal, Dan
5. Sincerely Pam — (greeting (closing)) — Sincerely, Pam

Answer Key

Page 64

End Marks

An end mark is the punctuation that comes at the end of a sentence.
Statements, or telling sentences, end in a period: .
Sentences that ask a question end in a question mark: ?
Sentences that show strong feeling end in an exclamation mark: !
   Riley is reading a book.
   What is the name of the book?
   I love that book!

Read each sentence. Write the correct end mark.

1. What flavor of ice cream is your favorite **?**
2. I just finished reading a book about dolphins **.**
3. That was the funniest joke I have ever heard **!**
4. When will dinner be ready **?**
5. Dinner will be ready at six o'clock **.**
6. I'll set the table tonight **.**
7. That bird just caught a fish **!**
8. Do you have time to go to the store **?**

Page 65

End Marks

An end mark is the punctuation that comes at the end of a sentence.
Statements, or telling sentences, end in a period: .
Sentences that ask a question end in a question mark: ?
Sentences that show strong feeling end in an exclamation mark: !

Rewrite each sentence with the correct end mark.

1. I'm going to be very late if I don't hurry
   I'm going to be very late if I don't hurry!
2. Did you see the full moon last night
   Did you see the full moon last night?
3. How many people will be here for dinner
   How many people will be here for dinner?
4. I will write my book report on Tuesday
   I will write my book report on Tuesday.
5. We're getting a puppy today
   We're getting a puppy today.
6. Are you ready to perform in the play tonight
   Are you ready to perform in the play tonight?
7. Yes, and I am very excited
   Yes, and I am very excited!

Page 66

Contractions

Some contractions consist of a pronoun and a verb combined into a single word. An apostrophe (') replaces the dropped letter or letters in a contraction.

Pronoun and Verb	Contraction
I am	I'm
He is, She is, It is	He's, She's, It's
We are	We're
You are	You're
They are	They're

Write the contraction of the words in the parentheses ( ).

1. Mrs. Murphy asked if **you're** staying for lunch. (you are)
2. **She's** making hamburgers and potato salad. (She is)
3. Tomorrow, **it's** supposed to rain all day. (it is)
4. Our cat is sick so **we're** bringing her to the vet. (we are)
5. **I'm** always on time for school. (I am)
6. The choir needs more singers, so **he's** going to audition. (he is)

Page 67

Contractions

Some contractions consist of a pronoun and a verb combined into a single word. An apostrophe (') replaces the dropped letter or letters in a contraction.

Pronoun and Verb	Contractions
I will	I'll
He will, She will, It will	He'll, She'll, It'll
We will	We'll
You will	You'll
They will	They'll

Rewrite each sentence. Replace the underlined words with a contraction.

1. <u>We will</u> meet you at the airport.
   We'll meet you at the airport.
2. Please tell me what time <u>you will</u> be here.
   Please tell me what time you'll be here.
3. <u>I will</u> see you when you arrive.
   I'll see you when you arrive.
4. <u>It will</u> be wonderful to spend time together.
   It'll be wonderful to spend time together.
5. If it rains, <u>they will</u> bring an umbrella.
   If it rains, they'll bring an umbrella.

Answer Key

Page 68

Punctuate Dialogue

Dialogue is a conversation between two or more characters. Quotation marks show the exact words a speaker says. Use a comma to separate the speaker's introduction or tag from the words he or she says. Place periods inside quotation marks. If the dialogue itself ends in a question mark or an exclamation point, place the punctuation inside the final quotation mark and drop the comma.

Tara said, "We must all have positive attitudes."
"We must all have positive attitudes," **said Tara.**

Rewrite each sentence, with correct punctuation.

1. Monique said I will start my homework after dinner.
   Monique said, "I will start my homework after dinner."

2. I hope you won't stay up too late said Mom.
   "I hope you won't stay up too late," said Mom.

3. I have a lot of homework replied Monique. I'll start now.
   "I have a lot of homework," replied Monique. "I'll start now."

4. Dad said I'll call you when dinner is ready.
   Dad said, "I'll call you when dinner is ready."

5. Thanks, Dad said Monique.
   "Thanks, Dad," said Monique.

6. Dad called Monique! Don't forget your books!
   Dad called, "Monique! Don't forget your books!"

Page 69

Punctuate Dialogue

Dialogue is a conversation between two or more characters. Quotation marks show the exact words a speaker says. Use a comma to separate the speaker's introduction or tag from the words he or she says. Place periods inside quotation marks. If the dialogue itself ends in a question mark or an exclamation point, place the punctuation inside the final quotation mark and drop the comma.

Alicia said, "We should all try to get along."
"We should all try to get along," **said Alicia.**

Rewrite each sentence with correct punctuation.

1. Cammy said Let's meet at the library after school.
   Cammy said, "Let's meet at the library after school."

2. I can be there at four o'clock answered Jake.
   "I can be there at four o'clock," answered Jake.

3. Tammy said I'm right here behind you.
   Tammy said, "I'm right here behind you."

4. Tom exclaimed I can't believe that you didn't call me!
   Tom exclaimed, "I can't believe that you didn't call me!"

5. Molly replied I was so busy last night that I forgot.
   Molly replied, "I was so busy last night that I forgot."

6. I'm sorry added Molly. I won't forget again.
   "I'm sorry," added Molly. "I won't forget again."

Page 70

Punctuate Dialogue

Dialogue is a conversation between two or more characters. Quotation marks show the exact words a speaker says. Use a comma to separate the speaker's introduction or tag from the words he or she says. Place periods inside quotation marks. If the dialogue itself ends in a question mark or an exclamation point, place the punctuation inside the final quotation mark and drop the comma.

Coach Jones said, "You are late."
"Why are you late again**?**" **asked Coach Jones.**
"I'm really sorry," apologized Frances**.** "I missed the bus**.**"

Rewrite each sentence with correct punctuation.

1. Can you help me make dinner? Sandeep asked.
   "Can you help me make dinner?" Sandeep asked.

2. Yes, I can help you Tal answered. What do you want?
   "Yes, I can help you," Tal answered. "What do you want?"

3. I want to see the new 3-D movie. said Wendy.
   "I want to see the new 3-D movie," said Wendy.

4. me too replied Jenny. It looks really scary!
   "Me too," replied Jenny. "It looks really scary!"

5. It looks as if it might snow said Mrs. Wu.
   "It looks as if it might snow," said Mrs. Wu.

6. I hope not replied Mr. Wu. I left my boots at home.
   "I hope not," replied Mr. Wu. "I left my boots at home."

Page 71

Punctuate Dialogue

Dialogue is a conversation between two or more characters. Quotation marks show the exact words a speaker says. Use a comma to separate the speaker's introduction or tag from the words he or she says. Place periods inside quotation marks. If the dialogue itself ends in a question mark or an exclamation point, place the punctuation inside the final quotation mark and drop the comma.

"How many children are in your family**?**" **asked Mr. Sanez.**
Angela explained, "I am the youngest of three sisters."
"I have one brother," Marco said**,** "and one sister**.**"

Rewrite each sentence with correct punctuation.

1. Erik complained There are too many leaves to rake.
   Erik complained, "There are too many leaves to rake."

2. Would you like some help? asked Raul.
   "Would you like some help?" asked Raul.

3. Helene groaned I feel really sick.
   Helene groaned, "I feel really sick."

4. Why did you like that book? Pedro asked.
   "Why did you like that book?" Pedro asked.

5. I was born in Russia Yuri explained. Where are you from?
   "I was born in Russia," Yuri explained. "Where are you from?"

6. I have to run an errand Mara said.
   "I have to run an errand," Mara said.

Answer Key

Page 72

Punctuate Dialogue

Dialogue is a conversation between two or more characters. Quotation marks show the exact words a speaker says. Use a comma to separate the speaker's introduction or tag from the words he or she says. Place periods inside quotation marks. If the dialogue itself ends in a question mark or an exclamation point, place the punctuation inside the final quotation mark and drop the comma.
  Bella yawned and said, "I'm too tired to read another page."
  "I'm going to bed, too**,**" agreed Roza. "What time is it**?**"

Rewrite each sentence with correct punctuation.

1. What time is the concert? Sam asked.
   "What time is the concert?" Sam asked.

2. It starts at 7 o'clock answered Liz. But let's get there early.
   "It starts at 7 o'clock," answered Liz. "But let's get there early."

3. Mom asked How many friends will be sleeping over?
   Mom asked, "How many friends will be sleeping over?"

4. Only Amar and Beto said Tony. Is that okay?
   "Only Amar and Beto," said Tony. "Is that okay?"

5. What time will you be home today? asked Uncle Arturo.
   "What time will you be home today?" asked Uncle Arturo.

6. Gino replied I should be home right after band practice.
   Gino replied, "I should be home right after band practice."

Page 73

Capitalize Proper Nouns

Common nouns name a general person, place, or thing. Proper nouns name specific people, places, or things. Each main word in a proper noun should begin with a capital letter.

Common Noun	Proper Noun
painting	Mona Lisa
park	Grand Teton National Park
sea	Caribbean Sea

Use the chart below to sort and match each common and proper noun in the box. Write each proper noun with correct capitalization.

state	harry potter	friday	main character
lake erie	continent	california	lake
fairy tale	day	the three little pigs	africa

Common Nouns	Proper Nouns
state	California
main character	Harry Potter
continent	Africa
lake	Lake Erie
fairy tale	The Three Little Pigs
day	Friday

Page 74

Capitalize Proper Nouns

A proper noun names a specific person, place, or thing. Each main word of a proper noun should begin with a capital letter. The titles and names of people; the days of the week and the months of the year; and specific holidays and names of geographic places are proper nouns.
  Groundhog Day is a holiday in **February**.
  On **Tuesday, Ivan** will visit the **Museum of Art**.

Circle the proper noun in each sentence. Then rewrite the sentence with correct capitalization for the proper noun.

1. Last summer, we went to (new orleans, louisiana).
   Last summer, we went to New Orleans, Louisiana.

2. The (grand canyon) is an amazing place to visit.
   The Grand Canyon is an amazing place to visit.

3. This year, we will celebrate (thanksgiving) at my grandparent's house.
   This year, we will celebrate Thanksgiving at my grandparents' house.

4. We saw many boats sailing on (lake huron).
   We saw many boats sailing on Lake Huron.

5. My brother wants to climb (mount whitney) someday.
   My brother wants to climb Mount Whitney someday.

6. On (independence day), we had a picnic and watched fireworks.
   On Independence Day, we had a picnic and watched fireworks.

7. Have you ever seen the magnificent (niagara falls)?
   Have you ever seen the magnificent Niagara Falls?

Page 75

Capitalize Book Titles

Capitalize the first and last word and each additional main word of a book title. Unless it is the first or last word of the title, do not capitalize the following words: **a**, **an**, and **the**; most short prepositions, such as **at**, **in**, **by**, **for**, **of**, and **to**; and conjunctions such as **and**, **but**, **or**, and **nor**.

Rewrite each book title with correct capitalization.

1. the sword And The stone
   The Sword and the Stone

2. island of the blue dolphins
   Island of the Blue Dolphins

3. robin hood And his merry Men
   Robin Hood and His Merry Men

4. charlie and the chocolate factory
   Charlie and the Chocolate Factory

5. tom swift, boy inventor
   Tom Swift, Boy Inventor

6. james and the giant Peach
   James and the Giant Peach

7. the wizard of oz
   The Wizard of Oz

Answer Key

Page 76

Sentence Types

There are four different types of sentences. The end punctuation reveals the sentence type.

Declarative:	statement, or telling sentence	ends in a period .
Interrogative:	sentence that asks a question	ends in a question mark ?
Exclamatory:	sentence that shows strong feeling	ends in an exclamation mark !
Imperative:	sentence that gives a command	ends in a period .

Read each sentence. Circle the sentence type.
Then write the correct end punctuation on the line.

1. Are you trying out for the team **?**
   statement (question) exclamation command
2. I don't know how to play field hockey **.**
   (statement) question exclamation command
3. I can teach you right this minute **!**
   statement question (exclamation) command
4. Hold this field hockey stick **.**
   statement question exclamation (command)
5. I'll roll the ball to you, and you try to hit it with the stick **.**
   (statement) question exclamation command
6. Shouldn't I warm up first **?**
   statement (question) exclamation command

Page 77

Fragments and Complete Sentences

A complete sentence contains a subject and a verb, and expresses a complete thought. A sentence fragment is missing a subject, a verb, or both, so it does not express a complete thought. To correct a fragment, add the missing subject or verb.
The baker a special cake.
The baker **made** a special cake.

Read each sentence. Write *CS* if it is a complete sentence. If the group of words is a fragment, write what is missing: *subject* or *verb*.

1. _verb_ The cows at the farm.
2. _CS_ That movie was hilarious.
3. _subject_ Made three snowmen.
4. _subject_ Might miss the math test due to the flu.
5. _verb_ Big, gray clouds in the sky.

Rewrite each pair of fragments as a complete sentence.

6. Every member of my family. Attended the reunion picnic.
   Every member of my family attended the reunion picnic.
7. My sister and her friends. To the local mall.
   My sister and her friends went to the local mall.

Page 78

Fragments and Complete Sentences

A complete sentence contains a subject and a verb, and expresses a complete thought. A sentence fragment is missing a subject, a verb, or both, so it does not express a complete thought. To correct a fragment, add the missing subject or verb.

For each fragment, circle what is missing: *subject* or *verb*. Choose a phrase from the box and rewrite the fragment as a complete sentence.

| fell | bloom | our favorite cousin | the ship's captain | a red truck |

1. Daffodils, irises, and tulips.
   subject (verb)
   Daffodils, irises, and tulips bloom.
2. Announced the news to the passengers.
   (subject) verb
   The ship's captain announced the news.
3. Invited us to spend the weekend.
   (subject) verb
   Our favorite cousin invited us.
4. The leaves swirling in the air.
   subject (verb)
   The leaves swirling in the air fell.
5. Is parked in the driveway.
   (subject) verb
   A red truck is parked.

Page 79

Use Coordinating Conjunctions to Form Compound Sentences

Use a comma and a coordinating conjunction such as **and**, **or**, **but**, and **so** to combine two sentences to form a compound sentence. The conjunction shows how the two parts of the compound sentence are related. **And** adds information, **or** shows a choice, **but** shows a contrast, and **so** shows a result. Always place a comma before the conjunction.
Do you want pizza. Would you prefer pasta?
Do you want pizza, **or** would you prefer pasta?

Write the correct coordinating conjunctions to show how the parts of the sentence are related. Choose one of the following: *and, or, but,* or *so*.

1. Sophia doesn't eat meat, _but_ she does eat fish.
2. Jose was feverish, _and_ he had a cough.
3. My brother likes fishing, _but_ he doesn't like hiking.
4. I might go to the circus, _or_ I could go to the movies.
5. Nino's bike had a flat tire, _so_ he couldn't ride it.
6. We needed butter, _so_ I went to the corner store.
7. Mr. Garcia plays soccer, _and_ he coaches volleyball, too.
8. I can walk to my aunt's house, _or_ I can take the bus.

Conquer Grammar • Grade 3 • © Newmark Learning, LLC

Answer Key

Page 80

Use Coordinating Conjunctions to Form Compound Sentences

Use a comma and a coordinating conjunction such as **and**, **or**, **but**, and **so** to combine two sentences to form a compound sentence. The conjunction shows how the two parts of the compound sentence are related. **And** adds information, **or** shows a choice, **but** shows a contrast, and **so** shows a result. Always place a comma before the conjunction.
  I enjoy skating. I like bike riding more.
  I enjoy skating, **but** I like bike riding more.

Circle the correct conjunction to join each pair of sentences. Then write the compound sentence on the line. Remember to add a comma where needed.

1. Carlos saw a movie last week. He went to a museum.
   (and)   but   or
   Carlos saw a movie last week, and he went to a museum.

2. I called my father. He won't worry about me.
   but   and   (so)
   I called my father, so he won't worry about me.

3. Kate can't come over now. She can come over later.
   or   and   (but)
   Kate can't come over now, but she can come over later.

4. Should I get a puppy? Should I get an older dog?
   (or)   so   and
   Should I get a puppy, or should I get an older dog?

5. I set my alarm. I'm sure I won't oversleep.
   but   (so)   and
   I set my alarm, so I'm sure I won't oversleep.

Page 81

Use Coordinating Conjunctions to Form Compound Sentences

Use a comma and a coordinating conjunction such as **and**, **or**, **but**, and **so** to combine two sentences to form a compound sentence. The conjunction shows how the two parts of the compound sentence are related. **And** adds information, **or** shows a choice, **but** shows a contrast, and **so** shows a result. Always place a comma before the conjunction.
  I like spinach. I don't like kale.
  I like spinach, **but** I don't like kale.

Rewrite each pair of sentences to form a compound sentence. Use one of the following coordinating conjunctions: and, or, but, so.

1. It was raining hard. The football game was called off.
   It was raining hard, so the football game was called off.

2. Omar needs new boots. He just bought a pair of gloves.
   Omar needs new boots, and he just bought a pair of gloves.

3. I speak Chinese at home. I speak English at school.
   I speak Chinese at home, but I speak English at school.

4. I might buy the book. I might take it out at the library.
   I might buy the book, or I might take it out at the library.

5. Rodrigo was thirsty. He got a glass of water.
   Rodrigo was thirsty, so he got a glass of water.

Page 82

Use Subordinating Conjunctions to Form Complex Sentences

Use a comma and a subordinating conjunction such as **although**, **because**, **since**, **while**, **if**, **when**, **before**, and **until** to combine two sentences to form a complex sentence.
  I love to visit my aunt **because** she is so much fun.
  I will visit her today **unless** practice runs late.

Circle the correct subordinating conjunction to complete each sentence. Write it on the line.

1. I will save you a seat _unless_ you get there first.
   although   (unless)   when

2. Harry said he was sorry _although_ I'm not sure he means it.
   after   (although)   while

3. Please come to the office _when_ you arrive.
   (when)   because   although

4. I don't have enough binders _because_ I used them all.
   while   although   (because)

5. Please try to be quiet _until_ the baby wakes up.
   (until)   because   while

6. I will wash the dishes _since_ you cooked dinner.
   before   unless   (since)

Page 83

Use Subordinating Conjunctions to Form Complex Sentences

Use a comma and a subordinating conjunction such as **although**, **because**, **since**, **while**, **if**, **when**, **before**, and **until** to combine two sentences to form a complex sentence.
  I loved the movie. It was really exciting.
  I loved the movie **because** it was really exciting.

Write the correct subordinating conjunction to complete each sentence. Choose one of the following: although, because, if, when, before, until.

1. Please stop at the store _although_ it's out of your way.

2. Sunita brushes her teeth _before_ she goes to sleep.

3. My dog sits at my feet _when_ I eat dinner.

4. Ken practices the piano _until_ he doesn't make any mistakes.

5. We can have a pool party _if_ it doesn't rain.

6. I did well on the test _because_ I studied hard.

7. I go to the movies _when_ the weather is bad.

Answer Key

Page 84

Use Subordinating Conjunctions to Form Complex Sentences

Use a comma and a subordinating conjunction such as **although**, **because**, **since**, **while**, **if**, **when**, **before**, and **until** to combine two sentences to form a complex sentence.
  We'll play softball **unless** the field is too wet.
  Our dog drinks water **after** he runs in the park.

Rewrite each pair of sentences to form a complex sentence. Use one of the following subordinating conjunctions: *since, unless, while, before, after*.

1. Amy can go to bed late. She is in third grade now.
   Amy can go to bed late since she is in third grade now.
2. I changed my sheets. I made my bed.
   I changed my sheets before I made my bed.
3. We can go boating. It stopped raining.
   We can go boating since it stopped raining.
4. You can't play video games. Finish your chores first.
   You can't play video games unless you finish your chores first.
5. We will go home. The actors take their bows.
   We will go home after the actors take their bows.
6. Stefan watched TV. His brother was having his eyes examined.
   Stefan watched TV while his brother was having his eyes examined.

Page 85

Compound and Complex Sentences

Use a comma and a coordinating conjunction such as **and**, **or**, **but**, or **so** to join two sentences to make a compound sentence. Use a subordinating conjunction such as **although**, **because**, **since**, or **unless** to join two sentences to make a complex sentence.
  Compound: Gabe loves to act, **and** he will be in our play.
  Complex: Gabe will be in our play **because** he loves to act.

Rewrite each pair of sentences to form a compound sentence. Use the conjunction in the parentheses ( ) and a comma.

1. My brother is good at math. I am good at English. (and)
   My brother is a good at math, and I am good at English.
2. It's a very long walk to school. I take the bus. (so)
   It's a very long walk to school, so I take the bus.
3. Lucas plays soccer. He would rather play the trumpet. (but)
   Lucas plays soccer, but he would rather play the trumpet.

Rewrite each pair of sentences to form a complex sentence. Use the conjunction in the parentheses ( ) and a comma.

4. Our tennis match ended. Then it started to rain. (before)
   Our tennis match ended before it started to rain.
5. We will also play tomorrow. We won't if the court is wet. (unless)
   We will also play tomorrow unless the court is wet.

Page 86

Compound and Complex Sentences

Use a comma and a coordinating conjunction such as **and**, **or**, **but**, or **so** to join two sentences to make a compound sentence. Use a subordinating conjunction such as **although**, **because**, **since**, or **unless** to join two sentences to make a complex sentence.
  Compound: Mina excels at math, **so** she may become a doctor.
  Complex: Mina may become a doctor **because** she excels at math.

Underline whether each sentence is compound, or complex. Then circle the conjunction in the sentence.

1. My mother is an immigrant from Spain, (but) my father was born in Virginia.
   compound   complex
2. My friends come from many countries, (and) I find it fascinating.
   compound   complex
3. I understand Spanish (although) we speak English at home.
   compound   **complex**
4. My family is diverse, (so) we have Spanish and American traditions.
   compound   complex
5. I am happy (because) we celebrate many different traditions, too!
   compound   **complex**

Page 87

Compound and Complex Sentences

Use a comma and a coordinating conjunction such as **and**, **or**, **but**, or **so** to join two sentences to make a compound sentence. Use a subordinating conjunction such as **although**, **because**, **since**, or **unless** to join two sentences to make a complex sentence.
  Compound: Ian waited for the bus, **but** it was late.
  Complex: Ian waited for the bus **although** it was late.

Underline whether each sentence is compound or complex. Then circle the conjunction in the sentence.

1. I love tortillas, (so) my grandmother often makes them for me.
   compound   complex
2. Many of my friends have pets, but Mom is allergic.
   compound   complex
3. I enjoy walking my next-door neighbor's dog (unless) it is raining.
   compound   **complex**
4. My neighbor across the street also has a dog, (and) I walk that one, too.
   compound   complex
5. I usually feed the dogs in the afternoon (before) I go to baseball practice.
   compound   **complex**
6. Baseball practice lasts for two hours, (but) today we got out later.
   compound   complex

Answer Key

Page 88

Compound and Complex Sentences

Use a comma and a coordinating conjunction such as **and, or, but,** or **so** to join two sentences to make a compound sentence. Use a subordinating conjunction such as **although, because, since,** or **unless** to join two sentences to make a complex sentence.

Compound Sentence: Felipe loves most kinds of pizza, **but** he doesn't care for olives.
Complex Sentence: Felipe likes most kinds of pizza **although** he doesn't care for olives.

Underline whether each sentence is compound or complex. Then circle the conjunction in the sentence.

1. I might be a doctor someday, (or) I might be a teacher.
   compound   complex
2. Mina will stay at the library (until) her mother picks her up.
   compound   **complex**
3. Eduardo will dry the dishes (after) his brother washes them.
   compound   **complex**
4. Nelly will shop for a dress on Sunday (unless) she is too tired.
   compound   **complex**
5. I will help Jack with studying, (so) he will do well on his test.
   compound   complex
6. The show started late (because) the lights were broken.
   compound   **complex**

Page 89

Compound and Complex Sentences

Use a comma and a coordinating conjunction such as **and, or, but,** or **so** to join two sentences to make a compound sentence. Use a subordinating conjunction such as **although, because, since,** or **unless** to join two sentences to make a complex sentence.

Compound: Jess likes to play basketball, **but** she likes softball more.
Complex: Let's meet at the park **unless** it rains.

Write a coordinating conjunction to complete each compound sentence.

1. Maggie ate lunch late, _so_ she wasn't hungry for dinner.
2. Violet is an excellent actress, _and_ she is a good singer, too.

Write a subordinating conjunction to complete each complex sentence.

3. I will be in the contest _although_ I'm not a good singer.
4. I kept eating raisins _until_ there were none left.
5. Andrea will join the team _unless_ practice conflicts with her trumpet lessons.
6. I asked Mom to pick up some snacks _because_ we were so hungry!

Page 90

Standard English

Standard English follows accepted rules of grammar, punctuation, spelling, and vocabulary. Nonstandard, or conversational, English is used in informal communication, such as in text messages, e-mails, and story dialogue.
Standard English: Lillian was very excited to visit her grandmother.
Nonstandard English: Lillian was gonna see her grandmother.

Rewrite each sentence. Replace any underlined words with the correct standard English word or phrase from the box.

| going on | Are you | hurry up | any |
| going to | have to | I will see you later | |

1. "If you don't <u>move it</u>, we're <u>gonna</u> be late!"
   "If you don't hurry up, we're going to be late!"
2. "I can't eat <u>no</u> more!" groaned Margo.
   "I can't eat any more!" groaned Margo.
3. "What's <u>up</u> with Dennis?"
   "What's going on with Dennis?"
4. "<u>You</u> kidding me?"
   "Are you kidding me?"
5. "I <u>gotta</u> go. <u>Catch you later</u>!"
   "I have to leave now. I will see you later!"

Page 91

Standard English

Standard English follows accepted rules of grammar, punctuation, spelling, and vocabulary. Nonstandard, or conversational, English is used in informal communication, such as in text messages, e-mails, and story dialogue.

Read the letter that Beto wrote to his Aunt Alison. Then rewrite the letter to better represent the conventions of standard English.
Possible answer is provided.

Hey, Aunt Ali!!! Week 2 at camp is AWESOME!! All the kids are super cool, and I feel like we're already best friends. This week we got to go camping in the woods, I thought it would be scary but we all sang so many songs and ran around and it was the best. Next week we're gonna ride horses! I'll let you know how that goes, I bet it'll be awesome too. —Beto

Dear Aunt Alison,
I just finished my second week at camp, and it was really great. I have already made good friends. We went camping this past week. I thought I would be scared, but we sang and played outside. I had a fantastic time. Next week, we are going to try horseback riding. I will let you know how I like it. I think I will enjoy it.
Love,
Beto